A NEW OWNER'S
GUIDE TO
TRAINING THE
PERFECT PUPPY

JG-109

Overleaf: Start with the best puppy that money can buy. Rely on the breeder's reputation and the consistent quality and health of his puppies. Here's a Boxer puppy bred by Richard Tomita of Jacquet Boxers in Oakland, New Jersey....just another future champion from America's number-one Boxer breeder.

The author wishes to acknowledge all of the wonderful owners of the puppies and dogs in this book. Their cooperation with our photographers makes this book possible.

Photographers: John Ashbey, Paulette Braun, Andrew A. De Prisco, Tara Darling, Isabelle Francais, Chet Jezierski, Janice A. Koler, Honey Loring, Linda M. McCarty, Vince Serbin, Robert Smith, Judith E. Strom, Karen J. Taylor, Richard Tomita, Wil de Veer.

Special thanks to puppy consultants (and *friends*) who read and re-read the author's original manuscript and gave candid and helpful advice: Barbara J. Andrews of O'BJ Akitas, home of over 200 AKC champions and America's most flawless Akitas; Nona Kilgore Bauer of Chance R Golden Retrievers, the prefix that means your Golden puppy got the best from the Best!; and Richard Tomita of Jacquet Boxers, home of over 200 AKC and International champions, the Boxers that define the standard. Each of these breeders is also the author of a fabulous TFH book on his or her breed in "The World of" series, and each book is truly definitive—caringly and expertly written and lavishly illustrated.

© 1996 by T.F.H. Publications, Inc.

Distributed in the UNITED STATES to the Pet Trade by T.F.H. Publications, Inc., One T.F.H. Plaza, Neptune City, NJ 07753; distributed in the UNITED STATES to the Bookstore and Library Trade by National Book Network, Inc. 4720 Boston Way, Lanham MD 20706; in CANADA to the Pet Trade by H & L Pet Supplies Inc., 27 Kingston Crescent, Kitchener, Ontario N2B 2T6; Rolf C. Hagen Inc., 3225 Sartelon St. Laurent-Montreal Quebec H4R 1E8; in CANADA to the Book Trade by Vanwell Publishing Ltd., 1 Northrup Crescent, St. Catharines, Ontario L2M 6P5 ; in ENGLAND by T.F.H. Publications, PO Box 15, Waterlooville PO7 6BQ; in AUSTRALIA AND THE SOUTH PACIFIC by T.F.H. (Australia), Pty. Ltd., Box 149, Brookvale 2100 N.S.W., Australia; in NEW ZEALAND by Brooklands Aquarium Ltd. 5 McGiven Drive, New Plymouth, RD1 New Zealand; in Japan by T.F.H. Publications, Japan—Jiro Tsuda, 10-12-3 Ohjidai, Sakura, Chiba 285, Japan; in SOUTH AFRICA by Lopis (Pty) Ltd., P.O. Box 39127, Booysens, 2016, Johannesburg, South Africa. Published by T.F.H. Publications, Inc.
MANUFACTURED IN THE
UNITED STATES OF AMERICA
BY T.F.H. PUBLICATIONS, INC.

A New Owner's Guide to TRAINING THE PERFECT PUPPY

ANDREW DE PRISCO

Contents

1996 Edition

7 · Dedication

9 · Perfect as Puppy Can Be

10 · Introduction
Like Mother, Like Pup •
Follow the Leader • Super
Puppy • The Social Creature
• Puppy and His
Environment • First Lessons
• A Leash on Life •
Come to Me • Play

46 · Crate Expectations
Making the News • Crate
Training Schedule • To Err
Is Human

Technicolor dreams.....

54 · Training at Home
Pet-Shopping • Record
Keeping • Not All Dogs Are
Born Equal • Discipline and
Training • Sit • Sit-Stay •
Come • Heel • Stand • Down
• Off • OK • Wait • Enough •
Here • Out/Drop It • Walk •
Night/Sleep

88 · Bad Habits and
Prevention
Crying • Nipping • Chewing •
Barking • Jumping Up •
Begging • Jumping on
Furniture • Running Wild •
Aggression • Digging •
Wetting

A Jacquet Boxer pup in training.

118 · Smarter Than Your Average Pup
Distinct Instinct

134 · Every-Day Things for Your Puppy
The Puppy and the Automobile • Grooming

Making your puppy bloom...

158 · Suggested Reading

159 · Index

Quality time with new friends.

144 · Glamorous Life of Dogs
Dog Shows • Obedience Trials • Field Trials • Tracking • Agility Trials • Sheepdog Trials • Schutzhund • Canine Good Citizen • Therapy Dogs • Instinct Tests • Versatility Programs

The making of a super dog...

DEDICATION

To Rick Tomita,

THE WORLD'S GREATEST DOG BREEDER

AND FRIEND.

ANDREW

PERFECT as Puppy Can Be

The dog is greed with a nose. A puppy can be perfectly puppylike, but livable, lovable and obedient too. It is we who choose to have these domesticated miniature wolf creatures in our homes. And we have a whole kennel of reasons to explain it.

As Rick Tomita, of Jacquet Boxers and Shibas, told me when I took home my first Shiba Inu, "Don't ever tell this dog, 'I love you.'" Those three little words can ruin all your attempts at training because your dog will always know that it is *he* who owns *you*. Even if you are doing the shopping, paying the bills, and cooking the meals.

The author's first dog, Jacquet's Tengu, as an unassuming six-week-old puppy. The Shiba Inu challenges even the most experienced trainer, who immediately recognizes the breed's cat-like trainability.

It's all about the upper paw! Dogs don't make ideal lovers. They are greedy by nature. They don't share. They're canines.

Sure it's fine to love your dog, and you'll want to share that last Cheese Doodle with him. Go right ahead and do it. Just remember—if the tables were turned, you'd never hear those three little words and you surely would never taste a Cheese Doodle!

Dogs do love their humans, but they're less sentimental and clingy than we are.

And then there's that nose! It's prominent on your puppy's face for a reason—it's his whole being, his brain and his instincts. We'll keep that in mind as we continue to learn what makes your puppy tick.

Since we've taken on these animals to share our homes with, it's time to mold them into domestic partners we can live with, and even love. As humans, we seek facts, fairy tales, and perfection, and our goal is to raise a puppy as *perfect as puppy can be.*

INTRODUCTION

A nxiety and fear of responsibility are two good reasons not to get a dog. Who wants to be owned by cuddly golden fuzz with sad brown eyes? Who needs scratched wrists, half-eaten couches and tattered leather shoes? Who doesn't like a full-night's sleep? Who wants a smelly kitchen covered by yesterday's news? Or a cat that won't eat and hides all day?

For better or worse, richer or poorer, in sickness and in health, you are suddenly avowed to an eight-week-old creature who doesn't speak English and acts like a dog.

A brand new home, exciting and unexplored; no other dog but me!; touch me, pet me, you're all mine!; my own room and all these toys; a bone for every day of the week; look how big my bark is getting; let's race around the neighborhood; is this a tree too?

The puppy is terribly excited! You are excitedly terrified.

Parental anxiety. Will I make a good parent for this new animal? What would my mother have done with this dog? What would his mother have done?

How perfect can a puppy be anyway?

Suddenly you're owned by a black and white spotted creature who's even more helpless than you are!

You can't wait until this perfect puppy is a dog, a real good dog? But puppies will be puppies, and it's a long rocky road until that perfectly irresistible bundle of fur becomes a companion, a reliable friend, a hunter or watchdog, or a champion.

Puppyhood is a full-time job...for the puppy and the family. Akitas require experienced owners who understand the importance of being the Alpha.

Humans forget that puppies aren't human. Face it, babies *are* human and they don't "catch on" until they're at least 18 years old. You've got to struggle through puppyhood—letting your puppy be a puppy, yes—for at least the first year of his life.

Not necessarily does this mean that your human life has to stop for a year to accommodate that new four-legged tyke. You must make certain sacrifices and be consistent about your commitment to train your puppy. The puppy's education is directly related to

Taking a break from playtime to snooze with a squeaky frog.

how committed you are to teaching him, and teaching yourself about canine thinking.

Since you can never get a dog to think like a human, so to speak, you have to learn to think like a dog. The world is different when you're on all fours, and lower too. And while the dog has been by man's side since cavemen figured out how to draw stick figures on walls, communication between man and dog isn't as sophisticated as Papa Evolution promised.

The lives of humankind have become increasingly more complicated with each passing century, and the dog has attempted to adapt accordingly. When man used to spend the day chasing pterodactyl, skinning prehistoric lizards and dragging his woman by her uncoiffed head—in the days when dinosaurs couldn't talk and weren't syndicated—the dog knew his place and his

With no antelope bone available, the Gumabone® suits this Rottweiler puppy just fine.

instincts fit the lifestyle. Man hunted the plain, the dog hunted the plain; man chased the buffalo, the dog chased the buffalo; man gnawed on a deer and antelope's leg bone, the dog gnawed on a deer and antelope's leg bone: life was simple and beautiful. The dog didn't need much training, and man didn't provide any. (A good thing since training books weren't available anyway.)

Time and technology have sped up twentieth-century life to the point that, to our dogs, it's one big indiscernible two-legged blur: computers clicking away;

12

It's a Frenchie-eat-Frenchie world out there! fax machines buzzing and talking; jets jetting from coast to coast to coast; collars zapping and invisible fences controlling and stinging an innocent nose.

It takes a pretty smart puppy to keep up, and there's nothing natural or instinctive about the ways of the world today.

Dogs don't read, and they don't talk to tell us what they're thinking or how they feel. And no, it's no revelation that dogs think and feel, despite what the *New*

Instinctual breeds like the Shiba Inu make superlative mothers. Fit and healthy mothers keep puppies spanking clean and always in order.

York Times Bestseller List tells you. They smile, cry, and pout too. Dogs can and do communicate, with each other and with us, the non-canines. They even communicate with cats and other animals, who seemingly have less difficulty understanding their signs and sounds than we humans do.

LIKE MOTHER, LIKE PUP

Puppies of course learn their first lessons in life from their dam, or mother; if their sire, or father, were available they'd learn their next lessons from him. In our modern world, the sire doesn't hang around the kennel where the dam stays. Very often dams are shipped to the sire's "kingdom" for mating purposes. In this day and age of supersonic jet travel, a sire's frozen seed could be sown and flown across the continent overnight. This father obviously won't have much to do with the rearing of his offspring. It is not impossible, however, for the father of the litter to participate in puppy rearing, though this may depend greatly on the breed of dog. As a general rule, the closer a breed of dog looks like a wolf, the more likely his natural canine instincts are intact. The German Shepherd, Akita, Keeshond and Shiba Inu are by far more instinctual parents than say a Bulldog, Chihuahua, Whippet or Neapolitan Mastiff. The more wolf-like

These Bulldog darlings put the capital "C" in "Cesarean"—a litter that could take even the toughest Roman emperor to his knees.

dog breeds retain a more natural body structure and therefore retain stronger inclinations to the wild. Akita fathers could behave more instinctively, more protectively, more fatherly. Man-made breeds like the Bulldog and Chihuahua are so superficial that they frequently need Cesarean sections and constant help through labor, whelping and puppy rearing. The females of certain dog breeds don't make very good mothers; the males therefore would make even worse fathers.

Mama dog, nevertheless, is truly in charge of the puppies' education: how to eat, where to "go" and when, what's safe and acceptable, and what's not. She is also able to correct her charges, and always does so lovingly and efficiently. Were papa dog still in the picture, he would take over by the fourth week and teach the pups how to play, how to hunt, what's dangerous, and how to protect themselves if necessary. The canine world has been "modern" in this respect for centuries: it was never the female's sole responsibility to raise the family; in fact, the female was always the head of the denhold, the dominant one and the survivor.

Although your new puppy is a mess-machine–piddling, tattering, crumbling and consuming anything anywhere– the dog is *instinctively* a very clean animal. Mother cleans up after the pups until they're able to crawl out of the den and then teaches them where to relieve themselves. Puppies upon leaving the breeder's premises should be housetrained inasmuch as they know not to mess in the place they sleep. We'll see that this is the only true basis for housebreaking a dog.

We can learn much about raising and training puppies from the example of the dam as well as from a basic understanding of canine behavior and instincts. This natural approach will guide us through that first difficult year we call puppyhood.

If your puppy is acquired from a qualified breeder, it should be housetrained (or nearly so). These Otterhound puppies know the virtues of cleanliness–an accomplishment for a dog as muddy as the Otterhound.

FOLLOW THE LEADER

Dogs weren't designed to live alone. In the wild, wolves exist only in packs, hunting together and sharing a communal existence. One dog must rise to become the pack leader in order for the pack to survive. For this reason your puppy will accept you almost instantly as a new member of his pack.

Socialization with the breeder makes the difference. This Golden brood is spending time with breeder Nona Kilgore Bauer, one of America's shining examples of the ideal breeder.

The importance of a puppy's learning to trust his pack leader cannot be overemphasized: it is the foundation of training a dog. Remember, previously your puppy's pack

Puppies need an Alpha to follow. These Jacquet Boxer toddlers have happily accepted the new leader of the pack, the young and on-the-move Roxanne Westra.

consisted of his littermates (unless he was an only puppy) and his mother; in some kennel situations there even might have been other dogs around during the socialization stages, or even a grandmother or aunt during rearing. Regardless, upon leaving his nuclear pack, where his mom was the leader, he is venturing out on his own and can quite naturally lead his own pack.

It's easy to spot the owner of a pack-leader dog. He's not the guy winning best in show at Madison Square Garden with his perfectly polite Poodle or dashing Doberman—he's your next-door neighbor being pulled down the street by his rambunctious "purebred" Lhasapoo.

If you're committed to giving your puppy his way about everything and letting him become pack leader, you can put this book down now because your job is an

Encouragement and training go hand in hand. With smaller breeds, such as the Silky Terrier, owners should neither over-handle nor spoil their dogs.

Puppies learn their limitations from their littermates. A full eight to ten weeks with its dam and siblings help to mold the well-mannered puppy.

easy one, though your life will not be. If, on the other hand, you intend to have a dog you can live with and love too, you better take control as pack leader right away.

Start off on the right foot: If you give your puppy a command or a reprimand (i.e., no), mean it every time! Don't go back on your intention. If it's no, or down, or sit, it's no or down or sit *now—* don't think that maybe next time the puppy will listen, because then for sure he will not. In other words, unless you're ready to deal with the puppy ignoring you, don't give the command.

Puppies are irresistible, and even more so, or so it seems, when they're disobedient or up to no-good. It is fine to let your puppy be a puppy. Accept what you can't change, as the axiom says. But don't let your puppy become a spoiled-brat puppy either. He will look to you

Puppies are not human. You must learn how to communicate with your puppy in a language that he can comprehend.

for the way, as he looked to his dam. Be there for him with instructions, expectations, discipline, and especially praise.

The pack-leader or aggressive puppy quite naturally assumes a dominant role, asserting himself and acting seductively macho. It is vital for you as his owner to show him that you are the dominant figure in the pack. Furthermore, he must understand that every human is dominant to him. There are a number of accepted ways to make a puppy subordinate to your liking. These methods are geared toward the dominant puppy at moments when he is acting up. The most elementary of these is lifting the puppy up so that he's facing you and his four feet are off the floor, telling him no, and suspending him there for a short while (about 30 to 40 seconds). A similar method is cradling him in your extended arms and holding him there until he calms down. Mama dog's most basic approach to discipline was the scruff shake: taking the puppy by the neck and shaking him. Although mama used her mouth, you can use your hand. This method directly communicates to the puppy. Always say no when the puppy is doing wrong.

How well do you growl? That's how your pup's mother expressed her displeasure, and mother knows best. Right? Since you're not a dog, you can't expect the puppy to accept your behavior and be able to translate it precisely to dog language. You may sound silly, and more so to your other family

Crate my puppy?! Just get over it. It's you who is conjuring images of doggy jails, not the puppy. The puppy thinks of the crate as his den, a place to relax or escape his uneasy owner.

members, but lots of the nation's top breeders confess that they do growl to teach a puppy. Your puppy may even assume you are playing with him, but if you take it seriously so will he.

The last resort to assert your dominance over a puppy is referred to as the dominant down. This technique can only be used on the most aggressive, insubordinate puppies, and not frequently. It essentially involves rolling the puppy on his side and holding him down by the neck and mid-body. This is the natural submissive position of the dog. Overdoing this technique can have deleterious effects on your puppy. Only use this technique in the most dire circumstances. Don't practice the dominant down—your puppy knows this is not a game.

SUPER PUPPY

Puppy ownership, sometimes thought of as puppy adoption, has frequently been compared to parenthood. In effect you do become the puppy's surrogate mom, and your family, his surrogate pack. Parenting a puppy is quite different from parenting a baby. Wouldn't parents love to "crate" a three-month-old and go out on the town on Saturday night? No such luck. Puppies are considerably easier to rear than children, plus there's no traumatic teenage dating years, college funds, graduate degrees or expensive weddings.

Parents today begin "training" their children earlier and earlier. Some tots are playing computer games before they're completely "housetrained." Four-year-old children compete for preschool entry and often need an eighth-grade education to get in. Parents of the children who get in—yes, yuppies—rush their Super Kids through childhood, opting to discuss Renoir and Monet instead of Crayola™ and Mattel™. Four-year-olds don't need calculus and Shakespeare any more than eight-week-old puppies

If your puppy has hunting dogs in his pedigree, he'll prove a better candidate for the field. The same is true with obedience and show titles as well.

need sonic collars and advanced utility training. Puppies need to be puppies—chewing on bones and playing with Frisbees®. So puppy owners can get carried away too, and why not?, with the world of purebred dogs as competitive, expansive, and expensive as it is today. While your puppy may never become an MD or PhD, he can certainly become a CD or TD; while there may not be a college fund, he may need several thousand dollars to acquire his championship; and while your bitch puppy may not ask for a huge Italian wedding, finding and hiring the right stud to mount her can cost the price of a nicely mounted rock.

If you select a collie from working-dog lines, you'll need more than lawn ornaments to keep him busy. This six-month-old Bearded Collie is blooming with talent and ambition.

Owners must have realistic expectations for their puppies, make smart choices about which puppy to buy, and follow through with the necessary training and education. Super Puppy is a dream that most breeders of purebred dogs have and never let go of. Before you purchase your puppy, you should know your intentions for the dog. If you are intending on showing the puppy and starting a breeding program, you will need to find a show kennel from which to purchase your puppy. If you want to find a Golden Retriever to train for field trials or if you want a Poodle to train for obedience competition, you will need to purchase puppies from established field or obedience lines. Much of the puppy's ability is hereditary. It is by far easier to create a Super Puppy from Super Dog parents. Most field trial champions beget field trial champion puppies; most dog show champions beget show champion puppies. Decide on your goal for the puppy and proceed with his training in a like manner. For

The real Super Dog, this is Champion Altana's Mystique who retired as the number-one show dog of all time, having won nearly 300 all-breed Best in Show awards. Her handler was Jimmy Moses, her owner was Jane A. Firestone.

instance, if you think you want to show the puppy, don't wait until he's three years old to enter him in his first dog show. Start that training early and be consistent.

The Westminster Kennel Club Dog Show is the premier dog-show event in the U.S. and is the oldest ongoing dog show in the world.

Most new puppy owners may not necessarily be preparing for that exceptional world-famous dog. Most readers may not even know that there are other valuable and famous dogs in the world besides Lassie and her Hollywood-trained offspring and a handful of other movie star canines. These Super Dogs are not fictional or comic-book creations, they are the progeny of very dedicated breeders and handlers who produce lines of dogs that produce champions, gain titles (which can be a five-digit expense) and win shows like Westminster Kennel Club or the Kennel Club Show at Crufts.

Best in Show winner of the 1996 Westminster Show is Clumber Spaniel, Champion Clussexx Country Sunrise, resting on his laurels. Owners, Richard and Judith Zaleski.

Perhaps our puppy will never see the inside of a show ring or graduate beyond basic obedience. Nonetheless, he will be a well-adjusted obedient member of the canine race. Very likely our puppy may be the sibling of one of these world-class dogs since about 80 percent of the dogs of any pure breed lead lives solely as pets. Not every pooch can be as famous as Lassie or Bang Away!

You, however, are looking to raise and train a puppy that you can spend your life with, and with whom you can share your love. Dogs are meant to be loved companions and helpmates, not headaches and unending expenses.

THE SOCIAL CREATURE

The basics of raising this puppy begin when you bring him home at around eight to twelve weeks of age. Most breeders release puppies to new homes at around eight weeks, though some breeders wait until ten weeks, believing that the dam's tutelage in those extra two weeks simplifies training greatly. It is true, however, that some dams lose interest in their busy charges by the seventh week and don't

Puppies accept people in much the same way as they accept other dogs. Socialization with children, adults, family and strangers prepares the pup for forthcoming life experiences.

make great educators beyond that point. Were papa dog around, he would intervene to relieve mama's load; in a true canine pack, other relatives, uncles and aunts, would also assist in the rearing and feeding of the young.

"Haven't you left yet?" After eight to ten weeks of nursing and teaching and pruning, mom is tuckered out and ready to allow her pups to meet new parents.

Socialization is the first priority with the new puppy. It is your job to expose him to all sorts of new experiences and environments in an effort to build his sociability and self-confidence as a dog. He already has the knowledge of how to communicate with other dogs, or at least other dogs whom he knows (his dam and littermates). He may not understand that there are more dogs in the world beyond his nuclear family. Meeting that first new dog will be an eye-opening experience, and every dog out on the streets may not be as happy to see him as his mom was.

Socialization with people is equally, if not more, important. The confident puppy welcomes the opportunity to meet new people. Depending on the

The human touch: puppies learn to enjoy people's company from an early age. These infant Boston Terriers snooze on a friendly lap.

breed, and the individual dog's personality, he may be head-over-wagging-tail thrilled to meet new people or merely tolerant of new acquaintances. No doubt the Golden Retriever or German Shepherd pup will greet each new person with a lapping tongue as a long-lost friend while the Akita or Chow Chow pup may merely nod his head and respectfully submit to the new person's hello scratch.

Responsible breeders spend much time socializing the litter, giving each puppy the time he needs to experience the world. Puppies are not unlike human babies in this regard: both need love and handling to develop properly. Some studies on human infants indicate that the infant that is never handled can literally die. Puppies, being equally social creatures, need an abundance of affection and petting to become touchable, lovable adult dogs. Unhandled young dogs tend to become overly shy and afraid of new experiences; some can even become fear-biters. Nothing is more important to a dog than his ability to bond. A dog unattached to any master is not a dog at all. Dogs need someone to love.

Breeders spend countless hours engaging the litter in people play. Socialization brings each pup out of his shell and makes him confident and trusting of people. These toddlers are Cardigan Welsh Corgis.

In order to continue the ten-week-old puppy's socialization, bring him to the mall or to the park, where there is commotion and people and fun noises. From eight to ten weeks the pup should be kept home to build up his confidence. Be sure the pup is inoculated before embarking on a socialization plan. Let him be handled by interested parties and talk him through these experiences. He should thrive on all the attention and have a great time. If you think you will show your dog, bring him to an outdoor dog show and walk around the show site with him. Here he'll meet a whole congregation of well-trained canines and their people. You'll also have an opportunity to get a feel for how the dog-show world works and meet people who have dedicated themselves to it. It is important that you keep the puppy on a loose lead for these outings. Not all breeds have a tendency to hang close to their owners. Likely most puppies will find the experience very exciting and want to explore everywhere fast. Don't rush the puppy through these experiences. Many puppies may find the outings overwhelming. Start with smaller-scale outings. Don't bring him to a 5000-dog all-breed show with a large gate and expect him to mingle.

Environmentally speaking, Labrador puppies are well-known activists...they like activity best.

PUPPY AND HIS ENVIRONMENT

While not every dog is ideal for indoor life, most are. If you have chosen an extremely large dog that is naturally protective, like an English Mastiff or Neapolitan Mastiff, you may not have the option of having him live indoors. You will not have to deal with housetraining, though your job of socializing the dog is no easier or less important.

You hopefully have chosen a breed that is suitable for indoors and with whom you can share your home. Do not give the puppy free rein of the house on the first day. Allow him to explore his area, which can be a kitchen sectioned off or a couple rooms. It is here that the puppy has his things (toys, bones, balls, etc.), his crate, and his feeding bowls. He should quickly get used to this environment and start to feel at home.

As a new puppy owner, you need to become a true "environmentalist"! Sure your puppy is against ocean dumping, the use of toxic pesticides, littering, and all kinds of pollution (even if his barking adds to the noise pollution in your neighborhood). In our context, the environment refers to puppy-proofing your home and grounds. There are every-day dangers that can cause serious harm or even death to your beloved charge.

While the immediate area in which the puppy stays should be basically danger-free, it is a good idea to examine your entire house just in case the puppy should wander without supervision.

House plants can be toxic to dogs, among the green things that can be harmful are Rhododendron, Philodendron, Dumb Cane and Dieffenbachia. Children's toys, such as marbles, jax, dice, and other easily swallowed objects, are very dangerous. Be sure that electrical wires are out of the way, under rugs, secured to floorboards, etc.

"The most wonderful time of the year"? Think twice before stuffing your stocking with a new puppy. Puppies would rather arrive on non-holidays...or bank holidays...or Arbor Day.

Christmas is an awful time for puppies. Besides the stress and the excitement of company and the like, the season invites a whole yuletide parade of well-costumed evils: burning candles, electric twinkling lights, ribbons, tinsel and garland, the holly and the ivy, mistletoe and those Poinsettias in full bloom, not to mention chocolate, turkey bones, broken glass ornaments. Plus riding in a one-horse open sleigh is no way to travel with a puppy...though it makes a great greeting card! He should be in a crate. Ho-ho-ho!

Medication bottles, cigars, cigarettes, ashtrays, home-cleaning products such as toilet bowl treatments and room deodorizers, and small sewing items such as pins and needles all must be kept from puppy's reach. And most pits are the pits, especially cherry and peach.

Antifreeze is attractive to dogs and deadly! Be sure to clean up thoroughly whenever you use it. Keep it somewhere your dog never goes. There are some dog-safe antifreezes on the market. These aren't widely sold at present but hopefully one day will be the only products available. Until then, dog owners must keep this sweet-tasting and smelling poison away from their dogs.

Detergents, corrosives, alkalies and acids, as well as paint products, should always be kept on high shelves. Be careful about where you put mousetraps or ant and roach "motels."

Chomping on a stick in the bug-laden grass, this Chessie puppy knows nothing of the nasty possibilities that await him outdoors.

When the dog is outside be aware of grounds that have been treated with pesticides, herbicides, rodenticides and insecticides. All these "cides" may make you wish you could just keep your puppy in-"cide" at all times. Other outside dangers include snakes, porcupines, squirrels, skunks, bats, rats and foxes. Any and all these critters are more fun than any Nylabone® could be—moving targets, real squeaky toys that fight back. Supervising the puppy at all times will help avoid de-quilling, de-stinking,

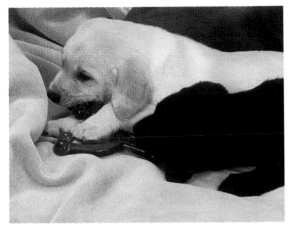

Taking a break with a Nylabone®....teething is more fun with a friend.

or de-treeing your puppy, not to mention the threat of rabies or poisonous bites.

The safety of your puppy depends on your responsible "environmental" position. Be prepared and informed. And don't litter either....and don't forget to poop-scoop!

First Lessons

At home with the puppy you should begin to teach him some basic commands. Of course the house rules must be stressed from the beginning. While the first word a baby learns is usually "mama," a puppy's first word is usually "NO"! No is such a wonderful word too. If possible, use the word in a positive manner (which sounds silly with the most basic of all negative words—be firm but kind). In other words, make *no* a learning experience, not simply a harshly shouted correction.

Since your puppy's natural instinct is to please you, make him understand that the undesirable behavior does not please you. Praise him instantly when he stops.

Do not overpraise the puppy during a training session. Praise is the key to training but it can also be misinterpreted as an invitation to get excited and play. You do not want to distract the puppy from the lesson at hand.

Bonding with your puppy makes training possible. Give your puppy a reason to want to please you and he'll obey and reward you forever. This is Rick Tomita spending time with one of the Jacquet Boxer puppies.

Training a puppy does not have to occur in planned sessions. A scheduled training time can lead to frustration for you and the puppy. If you lead a busy life, it can be difficult to find the time—no less at the same hour—every day. Train the dog, instead, at every possible moment. Short three-minute lessons will lead to a well-trained, attentive dog.

Mother knows best....especially when she's bigger than you. Mama dog never uses punishment—be positive and your pup will respond. Breeder, Richard Tomita.

Although you may not set up a rigorous daily routine, you need to be sure that you have "structured" time with your puppy. Structured time can be viewed as one-on-one time, a few minutes throughout the day where you stop, play with the puppy, talk to him, pet him, assure him that he's loved and that you can be trusted. This can be particularly important when you have more than one dog. Two or more dogs if treated as a "kennel" of dogs can become "doggy," more interested in dogs than people. With the hound or husky breeds, this can be a real problem, since they are already more pack-oriented than other dogs. Taking each dog out separately, to walk,

Two smiling female Pit Bull Terriers— an unusual situation captured with flair by photographer Wil de Veer. Same-sex pairs of aggressive dogs such as these rarely get on so amicably.

groom, or just bond, can make a world of difference in how that dog thinks about you, training, and life. Of course some dogs cannot be kept together. Same-sex pairs of dominant breeds, such as Pit Bull Terriers, Akitas, Airedale Terriers, and many others, should not be kept together. Dogs of these breeds constantly vie for the pack-leader position. Only in special situations can two of these dogs coexist peacefully. In certain cases, even opposite-sex pairs cannot be housed together. Quite simply, you may have to live with only one dog if you select a protective breed....but most of those breeds are enough dog for anyone!

A LEASH ON LIFE

Leash training should be a fun experience for the dog. Start with a lightweight nylon lead, not a chain leash. The puppy should already accept the collar since most breeders put collars on the puppies at three or four weeks of age. Check the collar regularly for size: the puppy is growing fast.

Different dogs need different collars. Use common sense and check the collar regularly to ensure that your puppy is not growing out of his collar.

While the puppy is in familiar surroundings (preferably indoors), put the leash on him and let him wander around by himself. Keep an eye on him so that he doesn't snag himself or topple a floor lamp or the like. The next time you try this lesson, hold the leash in your hand and let him lead you around to explore. The idea here is to not have the puppy panic when the leash is eventually wrapped around your controlling hand. Dominant puppies have a more difficult time on a leash than do the submissive follower types. Some puppies will scream; others will attempt to gnaw themselves free; others will sit and not budge. Be ready for any one of these reactions. Your puppy may do something completely different, more creative and very likely more amusing. Try hard not to let the comedian puppy entertain you to the point that you run for the Polaroid and abandon the lesson at hand (lest you'll soon have a very impressive collection of humorous photos of your one-year-old brat before you know it!). When the puppy does resist, by laying down, sitting, or just screaming, you must keep going—he'll soon recognize that his options are two (walk or be dragged). Once again, if you select a monster mastiff breed (Neo, Mastiff, Bullmastiff, etc.), you may want to teach this command before the puppy weighs more than you do.

"So this is a tree." The dog's nose is one of the miracles of nature...and gives the dog more information than he rightly needs. A young female Belgian Sheepdog bred by Linda McCarty sniffs out the bark.

When taking the puppy on his leash outside for the first time, begin slowly, letting him explore around in the direction that you want to walk. A brisk pace will likely be more effective the first few times out. This will limit the puppy's ability to dead-stop as well as to check out every tulip or fallen leaf in your neighborhood. Once you have gotten the puppy to the point where he'll walk without tugging or sitting or screaming, you can slow down and let him sniff around. The dog's nose is his first means to explore. It is unnatural to the dog to walk with his head up like you want him to. This must be taught. Keep in mind, also, that the male puppy will begin to discover the joys of every passing tree and every proverbial fire hydrant. This instinct develops slowly as he begins to notice the scents of other males on trees. Lifting his leg

Super puppies do not appear in every litter. This youngster grew up to be Champion The Widow-Maker O'BJ, one of the greatest Akita show dogs and sires of all time, owned and bred by BJ and Bill Andrews.

one day will come as a spectacular revelation, and the owner's joy in watching his little boy move toward doghood is equivalent to any father's son's first step!

COME TO ME

Teaching the puppy to come is the easiest and most difficult of all lessons. In theory, the puppy should like you and want to come to you. In reality, many things in the puppy's new environment seem more interesting to him than "dear ole dad." Call the puppy to you, bending over and using his name and the command *come*. Clap your hands, wiggle your fanny, smile a lot, and say his name like it's the password to Paradise. This is not the moment to be authoritative: use your happiest voice, your most playful tone. Don't be too far from him, else he may abandon his 30-foot haul to you for any and all distracting sights and scents on the way to you. Also be wary not to set yourself up for defeat by calling him while he's puppydreaming, chasing a moth, or otherwise distracted. Be sure you have his attention and then call him, and mean it! Don't let him ignore you. This is the most important element to not getting off on the wrong paw. For the cheerfully distracted student, offer a treat to entice him to come to you. There seems to be a mysterious correlation between easily distracted pups and chow hounds.

An enthusiastic game of chase with a puppy helps set the rapport between master and dog.

PLAY

This underrated and unsilly activity is vital to your puppy. To play doesn't mean to dally mindlessly and learn nothing. Instead, play means to experience the joys of your surroundings with those around you. In play,

Play time counts among a puppy's first lessons. In play a puppy learns limits, leadership and manners.

young dogs learn how to hunt, to protect, to defend, to spar, to hide, etc. Play brings out the personality of the puppy, a component of a pet which should not be overlooked. While breed standards describe the personality of a dog, no two dogs have the same personality. Some very giddy, near-uncontrollable puppies become the most civilized and aloof adults; other happy-go-lucky puppies remain the same throughout their lives. Playing games with the puppy—games are always a part of play—like follow the leader, hide and seek, fetch, catch, etc., gives the puppy new opportunities to react and play and be himself. When the dam plays with her litter, she engages in games to build confidence, to let the pups have a turn at leader, to win when the moment's right. As the dam rolls on her belly for a game of make-believe, the pups joyfully pretend to be dominant and feel what it's like to be leader. Although some dogs are natural followers, most pups will get a charge out of being in charge—if even for a fleeting puppy moment.

Fetch is a handy game because it tests the puppy's ability to concentrate and his desire to please. While retrievers, other gundogs, Poodles and many working breeds will fetch and return a ball or sock, other puppies will happily fetch, but the return part isn't naturally in their language. Frisbee® has long been a favorite, as is keepaway and other chasing games. Tug of war has become an unpopular game among dog people as it stirs a dog's aggressiveness and makes him rowdy around human hands. If a puppy is well socialized to human hands and is being handled properly, tug of war probably will not be harmful. Puppies love to play it with each other (usually with your favorite Rugby shirt). Admittedly, if you have a bulldog breed (Pit Bull Terrier, Bull Terrier, or Staffordshire Terrier), tug of war may fan his bulldog fires more than you may desire.

Don't be fooled that every dog wants to please his master. Many of the more aloof and independent breeds

Six-week-old Golden Retriever puppies roughhousing. Puppies take turns winning and being the "top dog." Each pup learns quickly that his littermate's teeth can hurt just like his own.

prefer to please themselves first and their masters second. Chasing a ball is fun and satisfies the dog's prey instincts, giving up the ball after the chase may not be rewarding to certain dogs. Your goal is to teach this puppy that if he gives it back, you can recreate the

Although tug of war is frequently advised against by trainers, it is a game that dogs engage in naturally.

*For games of fetch, the Nylabone® Frisbee® * is the right choice. Puppies prefer it because it smells good and is easy to pick up (from the bone molded on the top).*
The trademark Frisbee is used under license from Mattel, Inc., CA, USA.

chase part all over again. Though some puppies never grasp this idea, don't give up and don't chase the puppy with the ball or else that will become your game forever.

Playing games with a naturally alpha pup takes a self-confident owner, one who believes he is

Alpha dog must stay on top! Here mom has let her precocious pup go too far. It's time to regain her control.

the master. The goal isn't to crush the pup's will and drive, but to redirect it. Wear a quality antiperspirant: Never let him see you sweat. He must respect you, his alpha, who assures him that he's the best, strongest, biggest dog in the world, next to you. Often the alpha dog is also the smart dog. In order to keep the respect and attention of a dominant, smart dog, *stay one step ahead:* create more complicated play scenarios, keep him on his toes. Don't be repetitive: be creative, unpredictable, a little smarter than your brainy child.

If your puppy is not interested in games and is the shy crustacean type, it may take some effort to get him out of his shell. Don't spoil him and never give up on games. Be persistent and loving and he'll come around. Don't overdo it; go slowly but always a little faster than he's going. Be cheerful. Eventually he'll want to play more and learn from you.

Play ball! No matter the size, age or breed of puppy you acquire, playing should be a ball!

CRATE EXPECTATIONS

If your battle cry is "Crates are cruel!", you couldn't be more wrong or less informed about the canine race. Did you know that the vast majority of purebred dog breeders recommend that you purchase a crate for a new puppy? Crates are controversial in doggy circles. They are sometimes referred to as cages, which brings to mind unpleasantries like prisoners in zoos or laboratories. Crate is the preferred term, and the best of all possible crates is the wire crate, although some dogs prefer the confinement of a traveling crate (made of hard plastic with just a wire-frame door).

Let's think of the crate as a makeshift den. In the wild, dogs live in dens. Think of the crate as a condominium for your puppy. It's the only real place he can call his own: no one ever invades it and the rent's never due.

The crate should be kept in the central area in which the puppy stays. This is where he will sleep at night and at various intervals during the day when you don't want him underfoot. Regardless of your prejudice against crates, you will find that your dog actually *likes* his crate. Leave the crate open during the day and when he is not busy eating or playing or being a puppy, he will retire to his crate (or just go there to busy himself with a bone or his favorite toy or something he found and doesn't want you to see). That his crate will not be invaded is very important to him. It's security and privacy....

And it's safety. As any owner concerned with his puppy's well-being, you should consider that your puppy is always safer when he is in his crate and not eating house plants, knocking appliances on himself, chewing electrical wires, and the like. Do not put the puppy in his crate with a loose collar. He could very well snag himself on the latch, panic, and do himself real harm. A small nylon collar that fits should not be problematic.

So now he likes his crate, so what? He'd like a bed or a tattered chair as much, you think.

Crates are the most successful means to housetrain a puppy. Ideally a dog will not soil his den—that's where he sleeps, not where he eliminates.

Puppies inherit these instincts and will therefore never mess their crates. Keep in mind that the crate should not be too large, else the puppy may decide to mess in the "far corner" where he doesn't sleep. The crate should be just big enough for the puppy to lie down and relax. If you've selected a large breed, you can partition part of the crate off with a crate divider (available from pet supply stores)—in the long run, it's cheaper than purchasing a second larger crate.

Do not put the puppy in the crate for long periods during the day. He simply does not have the bodily control to hold his water all day. Not until he's six months old will he be able to hold himself for several hours. No dog can be

Safe, clean and private, crates offer it all to your puppy. After a week of crate training, puppies enjoy having a condo of their own.

expected to last through your eight-hour work day (no matter how mature or devoted he is).

If you are undertaking housebreaking the pup in the winter, or if you live in a colder environment, you may decide to put a towel or puppy blanket in the crate so that he can snuggle and keep warm. It is a possibility, though, that he may piddle in the terry cloth and crumple it up in the far side of his crate....and stay dry on the other side. Puppies aren't dumb, you know. This may only occur in a dire situation. The cool surface at the bottom of the crate would be more welcome to the puppy in the warmer months.

Consider leaving the radio on for the pup while he's in his crate. The sounds of human voices are soothing to him, even if they're not yours. Choose any easy-listening or classical music station. You want your puppy to grow up to have taste and to be discerning in all aspects of life. And besides, constant electric drums and guitars aren't good for his ears nor his peaceful mindset. As Shakespeare so eloquently puts it, "The man... not moved with the concord of sweet sounds is fit for treason, stratagems and spoils." Music calms the growing beast...in Venice, Belmont or elsewhere.

Trainers do not recommend using the crate as a means of discipline. Although putting the puppy in his crate after he has misbehaved probably will not have any long-term deleterious effect on the puppy—nor will it be as effective as sending a child to his room or a third-grader to the corner. Dogs don't understand punishment. They live for the moment and don't have a sense of remorse, in the human sense, that is. He will not hate his crate if placed there after a wrongdoing. Putting him in his crate probably will make you feel better for a while and give you a break from your industrious mischievous charge.

MAKING THE NEWS

Housebreaking means teaching the dog not to eliminate or urinate inside the house. Many people over the years have recommended the use of newspaper to train a dog. This method is not ideal unless you want the dog to use the paper for his whole life. If you have to leave a dog for very long days (up to 10 hours), you may have no choice but to paper train. You might consider hiring a puppy-visitor or a nanny or not getting a dog at all, if you really have so little time. Dogs do not enjoy being alone since they are essentially pack animals. It's no fun when your pack leader leaves you stranded all day.

As a housebreaking method, paper training is less effective than the crate. Consistency is the key to housebreaking—your consistency, not the puppy's. Keep this in mind during the housebreaking period: if the puppy does not respond in the desired way to housetraining, ask yourself, "What am *I* doing wrong?" It is you who's trying to accomplish this feat, not the puppy. He doesn't know that it's bad etiquette to urinate in the kitchen or on your new Aztec mats or Persian rugs.

Incidentally, smart puppy owners should avoid investing in new carpeting for at least a year or more. Why aggravate yourselves!?

While paper training is no one's favorite method of housetraining, in some situations it is simply unavoidable. For the individual who works out of town all day, the puppy simply can't hold himself for ten hours! The usual objection to paper training is that it codes a dog's thinking to believe that it's okay to relieve himself indoors. While an adult dog can hold himself for over six hours—he isn't happy, but he can do it—a puppy cannot. (Some dogs may even last ten—but you're really pressing your luck and his bladder. Bladder problems may develop in some breeds, like Dalmatians, for instance.) Eventually your puppy will be able to hold himself for over six hours, and by then he's already programmed to eliminate inside.

One concept of paper training is to line an area of the puppy's room with newspaper (six or seven sheets thick), ideally near a door that leads to "outside," and to teach the puppy that it's okay to eliminate on the papers. When the puppy goes on the newspapers, praise him like he's making the headlines himself! At times like this, we can't help but wonder if dogs think we're a little buggy. Clean up his mess and replace it with clean paper. There are a number of wonderful anti-dog-odor products available at pet shops. Be sure to clean the area well, else

Springer puppy makes the headlines! For some puppies, newspaper is the best route.

your kitchen or washroom will become unlivable, or at least unvisitable. You don't want the kids to say, "We don't want to play with the puppy—he stinks." Keep the room and the puppy smelling good. But there's a catch. Be sure to leave a small tatter of peed-on paper on the new paper so the puppy recognizes his scent and gets the hint that he's going in the right place.

Here's the fun part: as the puppy gets older, reduce the area of paper but *not* the thickness, so that he is eventually eliminating on just two full-size sheets. Remember that his puddles are becoming larger as his paper is becoming smaller. Don't skimp on the number of sheets or you'll be mopping the floor four times a day.

Praise him on harp and timbrel—whenever he goes. Hallelujah!

By lining the area in front of the door with newspapers, you can eventually place some paper outside the door and let the puppy realize the intended direction. You may have to pick the puppy up and take him outside when you detect he's about to go. Talk him through it, rub his tummy, run a hose in the background, hum the finale of Handel's Water Music, *anything* until he goes. When he goes outside, praise him till you gush! Isn't puppyhood wonderful!

If you expect your puppy to one day pee outside like a big boy, you must make an extra effort throughout the paper-training process to let him go outside so that he knows that's an option too. Some puppies never grasp that, and it's a real dilemma for the dog who tries to hold it through his hour-long walk around the park. In all likelihood, however, he'll smell the trees, bushes, fire hydrants, and park benches and figure out that some silly dog has been there before even though there's no sign of newspaper. Must be okay. At least I hope this is how your puppy will think.

CRATE-TRAINING SCHEDULE

We are going to set up a specific schedule for housebreaking with a crate and not stray from it. This is not as easy as it sounds, especially in the middle of a winter night when your fuzzy-slippered feet are freezing in the slush and you're waiting for your giddy puppy to stop building snow dunes and *"just pee already!"* Even then, you have to do it! Skipping a potty visit here and there can make housebreaking an endless, hopeless, smelly job.

Punishment has no place in housebreaking. Accept this fact and go work off your frustrations at the gym, on the tennis court or golf course, or on your significant other—not on your puppy. Be consistent and praise the puppy every time he does it right.

Early in the morning when the puppy wakes up, take him out of his crate and walk him. He should relieve himself before beginning his day.

Offer the young puppy a small breakfast and water and then take him outside once again to play and to relieve himself. Play should begin *after* the puppy has relieved himself. Don't rush the puppy inside as soon as he's done his business or else he'll learn to hold it as long as possible to maximize his play time.

Our method will be to take the puppy outside after being in the crate and after every meal. It may not be desirable to have a bowl of water available at all times through the housebreaking process. You can offer water with every meal and between them too. Let's not forget, what goes in must come out, sooner or later...probably sooner.

Put the puppy in his crate for a couple of hours in the morning. In the early afternoon, offer him his lunch and walk him again. Let puppy rest in the crate in the afternoon after he has played for a while.

By late afternoon you should take the puppy from the crate and play with him again, introduce training concepts, or just pal around. Feed the puppy right after this. Walk him after dinner and then let him rest for a while.

By mid-evening you should take him out and give him some attention, perhaps grooming time or a short training session. This is a great time to set him up on a table if he's going to be a show puppy.

Before retiring for the evening, walk the puppy once again and return him to his crate for the night.

The first night the puppy will probably cry. Some breeders recommend putting the crate in your bedroom so you can comfort him when he cries. Unless you plan to be there night after night, week after week, year after year, don't make promises you can't keep. Put the puppy to bed with his favorite Nylabone® or some other safe chew toy. Crate blankets or throws are available at pet shops and supply outlets. These items are ideal for making the crate comfy. Be ready to launder these if the puppy should have an accident. Unless he's not feeling well, this should not happen often. By the second or third night, he should sleep through the night and not cry when put to bed.

Don't think you can housetrain a puppy with no accidents. Be ready for them and remember not to blame the puppy. Visit the pet shop and get a puppy-repellent spray designed to cover up doggy odors. And have lots of paper towels handy. You should be able to see progress as there are fewer and fewer accidents with each passing week. Don't be distressed over a bad week in between when the puppy seems to have forgotten everything he has learned in the past weeks. It happens.

Remain calm and consistent and you'll be back on schedule soon.

The process should continue until the puppy is six months old. If you stop paying attention before then, you're going to find presents around the house that you weren't expecting. Surprise!

Puppy raindance in progress. Can you hear the drums?

To Err Is Human

Remember: every time the puppy goofs, it's your fault. Let's stop and consider the many mistakes you may make during housebreaking:

1. You skip a walk. Young puppies need to be walked four to five times a day.
2. You trade a walk for a free-style prance around the yard. Don't take for granted that your puppy took care of his business—he may have spent the time watching the neighbor's cat, chasing a beetle, or sniffing around. Walk him and you'll know if and when Mama Nature calls or not.
3. You leave him in the crate too long. Only if the puppy has been walked before bedtime and is really on "E" will he make it through an eight-hour night.
4. You sleep in on Saturdays. Don't. Get your eight hours and get going. Your puppy really needs to get out of his crate.....his legs have been crossed for an hour already and he wants so bad to be good!
5. You sleep in on Sundays. See #4.
6. You don't praise him like hell every time he goes! Don't take anything for granted. Not even dog poop.
7. You (or someone in your house...wife, child, lover, maid, the bird) overdoes the treats or handouts. This can disrupt the puppy's body clock. The crate is helping to "set" this clock, so don't confuse things.
8. You leave the water bowl out too long. A young puppy will piddle hourly if given the chance. Unless you want to walk around the block every hour on the hour, don't give him the liberty.
9. You let him have the run of the house. The key word here is "run." After a puppy runs, he naturally needs to move his bowels. Don't let the puppy get the "crazies" indoors.
10. You do not watch the puppy for "signs." If he is sniffing about, scratching at the door, or doing the puppy-raindance (in circles, of course), he is trying to tell you something. Forget the umbrella and get him outside.

No matter how wonderful and smart your puppy is, housebreaking will usually take no fewer than six months. Congrats to you and yours if you can do it by three or four months—you're exceptional! If you get lazy or overconfident about your little friend's control of his body, you are taking a foolhardy step (and don't forget to clean that shoe!).

TRAINING at Home

I f you think you and the kids are excited about the puppy coming home, imagine how that blossoming eight-week-old must feel. In a word, overwhelmed. Puppies have spent their first eight weeks with their dam and littermates....where everything is warm and safe. Puppies enter the world fully aware that they are pack animals. We must be sensitive to the puppy's needs as we begin to acclimate him to his new lifestyle.

PET-SHOPPING

Before your puppy comes home, you must raid the pet shop! There is a whole list of things that you must purchase before he comes home. A well-stocked pet shop is a veritable playground for the new dog owner. There's always a new toy, bone, or gadget that you'll want your puppy to be the first on his block to have.

Small dogs and big dogs alike benefit from having a crate to call their own. It's your puppy's "bedroom."

Let's start with the essentials:

CRATE. A wire crate that will comfortably stand your chosen dog when he's full grown. No sense collecting crates. Buy the right size from the start and purchase a divider to section off the larger sized crate.

STAINLESS STEEL BOWLS. Four or five just to be well stocked. They are superior to plastic bowls since they can be sterilized and nothing can grow in or around them.

Puppy gates teach dogs the limits within a household. Puppies and dogs accept the gate as one of the house rules and should not try to overcome it.

BOWL STAND. If you have a giant-breed puppy (Great Dane, Saint Bernard), a bowl stand is recommended to keep the puppy from overexerting himself by stretching his neck to reach the floor. These stands are recommended for deep-chested breeds as well, like the Boxer, Weimaraner, and Standard Poodle, because they keep the dog from gulping or wolfing his food and help ward off the possibility of bloat.

PUPPY OR BABY GATES. If you need to divide off a room or two, they are ideal. Pet supply stores offer a number of attractive options. They can be easily attached and make a safe haven for the puppy. Eventually, as the puppy grows taller and stronger, the gate becomes more metaphorical: he knows that he can climb over it, but he is trained to accept the gate as a rule.

NYLABONES®. There are a million bones to choose from on the market. Nylabone® makes the best 100! These bones have been around for many years, and they are the only quality choices. Even if they're more expensive than the other lesser-quality products, they'll outlast them all. Puppies *need* them for recreation as well as for clean teeth and proper tooth and jaw development.

LEASH AND COLLAR. These accessories are obvious. A training collar is necessary for teaching the puppy how to walk and heel. Do not purchase a metal choke collar as it will damage your dog's coat, especially if you have a medium- or long-coated breed. The nylon collars are far superior. A show collar, which is thinner and made of rope, is handy if you plan to train your puppy for showing. The leash should be 6 feet long and made of leather.

GROOMING BRUSHES AND COMBS. Depending on the kind of puppy you choose, you will need to buy the right brushes and combs. Most dogs will do fine with a natural bristle brush, but pin brushes, slicker brushes, and rubber brushes are handy on certain coats. Terrier puppies need a stripping comb. A fine-toothed comb or flea comb is irreplaceable for removing fleas. Matting combs are ideal for dogs with thick, heavy coats.

SHAMPOO/CONDITIONER. Any pet-shop brand made especially for dogs. Read the label, there are many quality brands to choose from. Some breeds, especially toys and smooth-coated dogs, require a mild formula.

FOOD AND SUPPLEMENTS. Follow the advice of the puppy's seller. It's best for the puppy's digestive system to keep him on the food he has been reared on. You can change the food gradually if you have a different brand in mind. Breeders recommend vitamin and mineral supplementation for certain puppies at specified ages. Many of these additives help to keep a potential show puppy's coat in prime condition. An electrolyte supplement can do wonders for coated breeds.

RECORD KEEPING

Take your puppy to the veterinarian for his first checkup immediately upon purchase. You should know which inoculations the puppy has had. Breeders commonly provide this information in written form to new owners. It's always good to establish a healthy rapport with a veterinarian of choice. Next to you, the vet is the puppy's best friend. If you find that your vet doesn't like your chosen breed, or maybe even your dog, find another vet!

An ID tag is IDeal for any dog. People lose dogs; dogs are stolen; dogs run away. Many communities have laws about dogs' being properly identified. In addition to the tag, which should have your name, address, and phone number as well as the dog's registration number, some owners opt to

For teething puppies, the Gumabone® is softer and more pliable, perfectly suited for tender gums and incoming canines.

have the dog tattooed (usually on the inside of his right rear thigh). The tattoo should be the dog's registration number. Microchip implantation has become another popular, reliable way to identify a dog permanently.

Keep your puppy's registration papers, pedigree and any other important papers in a safe, easily accessible location.

*"Why, oh Weimaraner!"
A Weimaraner can't
herd sheep like a Border
Collie, a Border Collie
can't run like a
Greyhound, and a
Greyhound can't hunt
like a Weimaraner.
That's instinct.*

NOT ALL DOGS ARE BORN EQUAL

You have purchased a puppy from a reliable source, have investigated your breed thoroughly, and have carefully considered the commitment of dog ownership. You are ready then to begin classes in thinking like a dog (or at least understanding *how* dogs think). Much of what a dog thinks is embedded in its instincts, heredity, and breeding.

Not all Shibas are created equal, but Shibas are definitely created superior to the rest, or so they think.

Not all dogs are born equal. Some dogs are naturally smarter than others, some more aggressive or outgoing, some stronger, etc. Understanding the dog's instincts and how the dog's breed or type affects his ability to learn can make your job as trainer simpler.

A pensive Pit Bull and a well-protected baby pondering the laws of Creation.

Pay attention. Here's a rundown of the world of dogs. Where does your dog fit in? If you have a crossbreed, he may "cross" over to a couple different categories.

TERRIER dogs, bred to go to ground to exterminate land pests, have strong digging instincts and tend to be tenacious. The degree of tenacity varies from breed to breed and line to line, but you can be sure that it is a quality which guaranteed the terrier's survival when faced with a cornered rat or fox. The terrier

Uniquely motivated, terriers have a "just do it" attitude and may appear stubborn and uncooperative if you harass them with too many commands.

breeds that have long been bred for show dogs prove to be less stubborn than the working breeds. Obviously Scottish, Yorkshire, and Norwich Terriers, for example, will be more easily trained than Rat Terriers or Patterdale Terriers. In truth, terriers have little trouble learning commands and understanding what is expected of them; they don't obey you readily. These dogs will require as much patience as they have persistence.

Terriers—or earth dogs—are territorial and feisty with each other. These two Airedales, the tallest of the terriers, are slugging out their differences.

SHEEPDOG breeds, such as the Border Collie, German Shepherd Dog, and Belgian Tervuren, have been bred to maneuver sheep, usually with the instructions of a human shepherd. These dogs can follow up to a

Keeping the flock together is the blessing of the shepherd dog, whether the flock be human or ovine.

hundred commands (hand signals or a combination of hand signals and whistles). They are eager to please but indeed are free-thinkers as well. The Border Collie many consider to be the smartest of all dogs. One facet of the shepherd personality that makes these dogs

The most intelligent of all canines, the Border Collie performs his bred-for duties with precision and determination.

ideal students and companions is the propensity to bond closely with their "flock," family, or pack. These dogs will do anything for you and absolutely adore the verdant pastures you walk on.

MASTIFF breeds, such as the Rottweiler, English Mastiff, and Bullmastiff, tend to be dominant and aggressive dogs. They require firm, consistent handlers whom they can respect. Before these dogs reach adolescence (and all the mass that comes with it), they need to learn to suppress some of their protective, dominant nature lest they become too much to handle.

Mastiffs are chosen for the size and power of their bodies over their brains. Many trainers find the mastiff breeds just as intelligent as many other dogs.

The Neapolitan Mastiff puppy is limited more by his mass and awkwardness than by his brain power.

These dogs can be alarmingly intelligent and learn their lessons with few repetitions. A bored mastiff is one big inattentive student and a major blow to your ego. Keep lessons short and don't tire him with too many review sessions.

SPITZ and husky breeds tend to be independent and not geared toward pleasing a master. The husky's work involved pulling barges and sleds and in effect was strongly pack-oriented. Humans are usually less interesting companions than other dogs, and these dogs resultantly require more energy to command their attention. Sled dogs never depended on humans for very much, except an occasional fish and an affectionate "mush."

Siberian Huskies were bred to haul goods over long distances of ice and snow. Today Huskies are more likely seen building snowmen than hauling sledges over the tundra.

Likely the most affectionate of the spitz breeds, the Samoyed pup bonds quickly with an adoring human.

Water retrievers such as the Chesapeake Bay Retriever can outswim and outrun most Olympic athletes. The Chessie's broad, strong head makes him able to retrieve and carry large game such as duck and pheasant.

GUNDOGS—retrievers, cockers, flushers and springers—have been bred to work from man's hand and gun. They are extremely obedient and live to obey and please their masters. These dogs can be trained to do amazing things and are programmed to work long days in the field. Hunting dogs tend to be easily distracted when outdoors as every twitter and flutter grabs their eyes and nose and pointer. Trainers recommend starting lessons indoors, where the atmosphere is

The Vizsla ranks high among the all-purpose gundogs. Like most other gundogs, Vizslas possess superior intelligence and exceptional trainability.

more controlled. Additionally, make sure they have been exercised sufficiently before attempting to keep their attention on an obedience lesson.

SCENTHOUNDS, such as Beagles, Bassets, and Foxhounds, tend to be slower to learn. The heavier hounds, like the Bloodhound, lack urgency and work in a more deliberate fashion. Though slower to execute tasks and commands, hounds are not necessarily unintelligent, just uninterested. They are not naturally clean animals

A running pack of little French hunters: the Petit Basset Griffon Vendéen makes friends easily, especially with other PBGVs!

as they have been raised for generations as outdoor kennel dogs—not indoor companions who act timely and tidily. Housebreaking poses real challenges. They are very nose-oriented and can be as distracted by the scents of

A low-key, low-legged hound dog, the Basset Hound puppy can be both profound and stubborn.

the great outdoors as a gundog is by a cotillion of wounded pigeons. Nevertheless they are good-hearted dogs with much to offer a patient, creative owner.

GREYHOUNDS and the other sighthound breeds are quite aloof and must be trained with extreme sensitivity. Harsh treatment or punishment could ruin a potential student. They are high-energy dogs and need fair amounts of daily exercise before you can expect to train them. They are keenly aware of "prey" and will bolt in a "split-hare" of a second. Most are very gentle and expect to be treated as objects of worship.

The eyes of the sighthound see far and well. The Whippet wins most races and is always a mile ahead of a lagging owner.

Dressed to run, these Greyhounds enjoy their title of the fastest canine on earth.

TOY breeds vary a great deal depending on their upbringing and origin. To generalize, toys tend to be spoiled and their training must begin early and be instilled with great care. Many of the toy breeds have a high degree of dependence on their masters, yet these same dogs are the first to become overly dominant. Firm but kind discipline is key to teaching a

A toy dog can fit into any household. The full-coated Pomeranian is a miniature spitz dog who likes the plush life.

Not a true toy, the Bichon Frise is a true doll—not made of porcelain, he is a sturdy, medium-small dog with the perfect temperament for children and adults.

toy dog. They are smart little dogs who can become destructive and deathly bored if not attended to and trained.

CROSSBREEDS or mixed breeds, dogs of unknown heritage or of two known pure breeds, are more difficult to evaluate though it is commonly believed that the dog will demonstrate the behavior patterns of the breed it more closely resembles. A crossbred Beagle-Bedlington Terrier that looks more like a Beagle will act more like a Beagle. Most mongrels or mixed breeds can be categorized as resembling a type of dog, if not a particular breed. Therefore a mongrel that looks like a terrier will likely act like a terrier; a mongrel that looks like a spaniel will act accordingly. Unfortunately, the mixed breed's genetic pool may be so varied and muddied that little can be predicted with any certainty.

Other factors that affect a dog's ability to be trained are individual personality, upbringing and socialization, exercise level, diet, and even his horoscope and mood. Likewise, the trainer's personality, mood, knowledge, and commitment can make a big difference in the training of the puppy. Perhaps even the trainer's horoscope affects the success of training. It's not likely that a dominant Leo trainer will do well with a sensitive, easily discouraged breed (like a Saluki or another sighthound), he'll do better with a mastiff breed. The Salukis are better with the creative, sensitive Cancer trainers, who may do well with spitz breeds as well (who require ingenuity and originality to train). Obviously, Taurus trainers do best with the bulldog breeds; kind and gentle Libra trainers sail best with easygoing sighthounds

Mutts get a bum rap! Although you never know quite how big they'll grow, you can expect that they'll be healthy and loving dogs.

A strong-willed dog needs a strong-willed owner. This leather-clad toddler is ready to tether and tame his brawny Staffordshire pal.

or calm toy breeds; Capricorn, the goat, trainers, may take to any of the herding breeds; indecisive Pisces trainers should probably avoid most breeds and settle on a goldfish.

Back from the stars...How friendly is your puppy? Is he dependent, shy, or nervous? Is he hyperactive or excitable? The personality of your puppy can positively or negatively affect his desire to learn and his attention span. Alert friendly dogs are easier to train than shy or unruly dogs. The strong-willed or aggressive dog requires a firmer hand than the easygoing, calm dog or the naturally attentive one. The stubborn dog requires crafty owners who are persistent and not easily outsmarted. The independent dog needs to be showered with petting and love to nurture his trust and appreciation of his master. The lazy puppy needs an enthusiastic owner to motivate

Patience and praise are the Bulldog's two favorite words! Young puppies need considerate owners who have the time to invest in learning about the pups' personalities and their breed. him and to get him excited about learning—ask any teacher in the school system for pointers and a lesson plan.

Every dog, no matter what his personality and heredity, requires a patient trainer who cares enough to get to know the dog and find the training approach that is best for the individual dog.

DISCIPLINE AND TRAINING

Training should be simple and enjoyable. Don't pressure the puppy by expecting too much of him all at once. Remember that he is an immature creature, physically and emotionally. To your advantage is his likely desire to please you—the most important first ingredient in any lesson. Don't attempt to teach more than one command at a time. The puppy's attention span is delightfully short. At eight or nine weeks, a puppy may pay attention for less than five minutes on a good day. This will grow with time. Be patient and enjoy your dog's puppyhood.

Always indicate on which of your shoes your puppy is allowed to grind his growing choppers. Like the rest of us, if given the choice, he'll choose the red pumps!

Every time the puppy does something right, praise him. Every training book in existence recommends lavish praise! So does this one—why argue with success?

Consistency is another virtue upon which to build your training. Set up house rules that the puppy encounters on a daily basis: we don't urinate in the house; we don't sit on the furniture; we don't eat mommy's macramé; etc. Changing your stance on any rule will only serve to confuse the puppy who is already trying to remember whether it was the furniture or the macramé he wasn't allowed to eat! Everything for a puppy is new, and he can be easily overwhelmed without your being inconsistent or wishy-washy.

Do not initiate training sessions when the puppy is wound up and hasn't had time to run off some steam. Let the puppy get his exercise and play first. Why compete with all that puppy energy? This is especially true of teaching the puppy to heel. You don't want to come home with a half-hanged puppy after his first heel lesson.

If you hope to have a well-trained puppy, you must realize from the beginning that punishment has no place in dog training. Correction, on the other hand, does. By correction we mean that the dog is told *no* in the midst of doing wrong.

You create "the dog." Your puppy is an empty slate, sometimes with spots on it.

For example, the child, playing in his room minding his own business, is disrupted by a manic mother brandishing a wooden spoon and screaming. The child has no idea that his mother just found out about the sandbox incident or laundry-soap catastrophe from the day before. Or does he? Puppies aren't human...

Scolding a puppy three minutes after finding the pile in the playroom or your chewed-up Hush Puppies™ means nothing to the puppy. You might literally have to catch him in the act. Some behaviorists have speculated that you have seven and a half seconds to correct the behavior or it's forgotten. Many trainers believe that a puppy can recognize his wrongdoing if he's marched over to the pile and told *no*. He will at least realize that something is wrong here. How he connects his scent to your screaming is not entirely clear. Likely, if you showed him the ex-Hush Puppy, he'll think you no longer like that shoe. Perhaps an Italian boot next time?

Somehow quite suddenly you are treating the puppy unkindly—and for reasons completely unbeknownst to him. If you can catch the puppy in the act, you may be able to punish him by isolating him for a half hour. This

has been recommended by many trainers. While it is true that puppies hate being ignored, it is not clear whether the puppy

Innocent until proven guilty! "Ah, to be young and democratic," quoth the Rottweiler.

associates his past action with his present state of unhappiness. Dogs truly live in the moment. They cope with the moment they're in. Dogs do not worry in the same way that people do.

How do you correct a puppy when "no" isn't enough? For sure, smacking the puppy with your hand, swinging a newspaper, or hurling the closest house plant are *not* options. Under no circumstances should you ever hit a dog. This does not communicate with the animal. His mother did not hit him. Your options are a stern *no*, a shaker-can (easy enough to make with a tin can and a pawful of pebbles—shake it briefly at the canine offender while saying *no:* all dogs hate the racket) and in dire situations, shaking the puppy by the scruff of his neck as his mother would have done. A leash correction, of course, involves a firm tug on the leash to redirect the puppy's attention.

If you are consistently encouraging and loving toward your pup, a stern NO will make him realize that he is displeasing you.

Regardless of how you correct the puppy, the single most important part is praising the puppy after you have reprimanded him. Dogs do not learn from the negative— NO—they learn only from being praised for doing right and learning what is not acceptable. As soon as the dog stops barking, digging, or jumping, tell him he is good.

The canine kiss means that he acknowledges your dominant role. Don't be grossed out: grin and enjoy your role as top dog.

To enhance your communication with your dog, you must understand how the dog thinks in order to interpret his body language and to acknowledge what he can and cannot readily understand. We know that the dog will never "speak" your language, nor can you exactly convey his own—even if you're a great growler. Instead use your own language in the most dog-effective way. Choose simple one-syllable words to deliver your commands (no, come, sit, stay, heel, down, shake, paw, etc.). Ideally you should choose a name for your dog that is or can be shortened to two or three syllables. It is irreversibly dumb to choose an eighteen-wheeler canine name that you can never pronounce quickly. As T.S. Eliot muses, even Asparagus used the callname Gus. Finally, while you know that dogs cannot understand the words humans speak, they can recognize our tone of voice. They are remarkably sensitive to excitement, anger, apprehension, and praise in your voice. It is arguable that a dog can grasp the gist of a complete sentence if spoken to him in a tone of voice he recognizes.

When calling the dog, raise the inflection of your voice

to get his attention. Make it bright and lively and he will pay you mind. When giving a command that doesn't require him to move, use a middle or low register (e.g., stay, down). For commands such as come or sit, your tone needs to be higher so he's attentive and ready to execute the command.

Following the master is the way to go. Make the come exercise exciting and fun and begin the puppy at a very young age. Breeder, Dawn Martin.

The immortal question "Does my puppy love me or just my cheese snacks?" has plagued man for time immemorial. Who cares as long as the puppy is obeying and happy!

Food rewards during training are a personal decision on your part as trainer. Many believe that the dog should obey a command for the sake of obedience to his master, because he wants to please you and not because he wants the Swiss cheese in your right fist. Everyone must confess, however, that food rewards work! Since training requires so much repetition of commands and exercises, food rewards make learning less thankless. Of course, his master's praise should be his prime motivation, but for some dogs praise alone simply is not enough. In time, the dog will execute his commands without need of any reward, whether it's a tidbit or a pat on the head.

Surely there are a hundred puppy and dog training books on the market today. Is there anything more daunting and confusing than the training primer that

Are you sure you have the puppy's attention? If not, you might as well squat and do it yourself!

reads like a complicated recipe and makes you fall over your puppy like you're playing Twister™? We will not give you a step-by-step guide to the necessary commands. Instead we will discuss the goal of the exercise, what pitfalls to look out for, and the various theories recommended by top trainers.

Remember that training should take place when the dog is both well rested and exercised. Keep lessons short and sweet. Praise the puppy for every little thing. Be consistent and mean what you say. Don't settle for a half-executed command. Always end lessons on a positive note or else your puppy will begin to dread and resent training time. Training should be fun, and your puppy should look forward to his lessons because they're time spent with his favorite person: YOU! But remember, training is serious business; lessons and play are two distinctly different things.

It is important for one person to train a puppy, not the whole family. Training the puppy is not like dividing up the daily chores. Always be the pack leader, especially when training your dog. He needs a teacher who is convincing and commanding.

SIT

The most common method to teach *sit* is to give the command while holding a food treat over the puppy's head until he sits to see it, then rewarding him with the tidbit and lots of praise. Soon he'll recognize the sit command without your having to hold the tidbit over his head. Another method involves giving the command *sit* and pushing the dog's rear end down.

Always stay in front of the puppy. Praise him once he's assumed the sit position for a few moments. Don't overdo it or he'll get excited and think it's time to play.

For some dogs this may be the less effective method of the two as it is not advisable to touch the dog during the lesson. Many dogs resent being touched where they can't see. These dogs will squirm when you touch their rear ends.

While the sit may be the most basic command to teach a dog, some trainers do not recommend teaching a show dog to sit since show dogs are often first taught to stand. A show puppy that sits in the ring every time he is presented with a tidbit can be problematic.

SIT-STAY

Always remember that when you say *stay*, don't move back. The puppy's instinct is to follow you. The command is given to the puppy when he is already sitting. Once the puppy has learned to stay you can move back slowly and repeat the command so that he understands. An effective hand signal for this command is showing the puppy your palm, like a traffic officer would to say stop. You can also use the stay command when the puppy is standing. Stay is one of the most important commands to teach a dog—for obvious reasons, it can save his life.

Accustom the puppy to the leash and collar before you attempt to teach a command. Some puppies take longer to adjust to restriction than others.

Call the puppy by name and praise him lavishly for coming when called. He should learn that you are the source of praise and food and other fun stuff too.

COME

The come command requires good attention on the part of the dog. (It helps if your puppy likes you.) The socialization part of early training will help to strengthen the bond between you. Clapping your hands is one way to get the dog's attention. Use his name whenever giving the come command. Using a tidbit is also a good incentive to get the dog to come.

HEEL

Dogs prefer to walk with their noses on the ground so that they don't miss any important smells. To get a puppy to walk next to you, at your knee, with his head up takes a bit of convincing. Your job is to convince the puppy to do this. Your initial attempts at leash training have hopefully been successful. Before beginning the serious business of heel training, the puppy should be accustomed to the collar and leash and to puttering about and following you. While teaching the heel, it is only sensible that you talk him through it and pat your knee to keep his attention and nose up. Keep up a good pace to encourage his attention. Let's use a sidewalk or parking lot for the first few lessons. A grassy field or lawn simply is too distracting for a young puppy—all that enticing good-smelling stuff. The nylon collar can be tugged if necessary to keep him in check. Use the word *heel* with each correction. If the puppy is ignoring your attempts or is overly excited, stop, quiet him down, and start over. Offer a food treat every so often. Keep the dog calm and under control. Make it an enjoyable experience for the dog.

Walking may not be as simple as you think. Some pups need more coaxing than others. Never pull the puppy—walking should always be a fun time for both of you.

Walking at heel will make all the difference in the world to your attitude toward walking your dog on a daily basis. A good heeler is a pleasure to walk; a puller is a real drag, so to speak.

STAND

This command is useful for the well-behaved dog: for allowing the vet to inspect; for standing to meet new people; for cleaning his muddy paws; for standing during a bath. Stand is also the command for a puppy that you hope to exhibit in a dog show. All dogs must stack for the judge, which means stand in a certain way so that they can be viewed and inspected. The dog

If you're planning to show the puppy, teach him to stand in a "stacked" position. This is professional handler James P. Taylor setting up an O'BJ Akita puppy—as easy as it looks, it's in the blood.

must hold this stance for an extended period of time when in the show ring. Bait the puppy with a food treat or squeaky toy to get his attention. Don't let him jump up. Say no and place him back on the floor. For smaller puppies and toy breeds, this lesson is best executed on a grooming table or countertop with a nonslip surface. Acclimate the puppy to the table first so that he is not fearing for his life. Show puppies must be accustomed to being touched, and allowing strangers to open their mouths and check their teeth, to run their hands down their backs, and to check the testicles of male puppies. You should do these things with your puppy to get him used to being touched. Always praise the puppy and encourage him to like handling. Hand-shy puppies do not do well in the show ring, nor do they enjoy it.

DOWN

Down is a simple and easy command that every dog must know. *Down* indicates a position with the front legs extended and the dog's body flat to the floor—you might think of it as "lie down." Don't confuse this command with *off*, which tells your dog to get down from you, a guest, or a sofa. Have your dog in a sit position, pat the floor and say *down*. Out of curiosity your puppy may

Ideally the puppy will assume the down position without your having to touch him. A treat will encourage him to stay and wait until you release him.

stretch to touch your hand or sniff it—this is the down position. Some trainers incorporate a treat to get his attention. Praise him briefly. If he doesn't react to your patting the floor, gently take his front paws and pull them forward.

Once the puppy is in the correct position, tell him to stay. The down-stay you will regard as the most useful of commands. This is a comfortable position for the dog and it can keep him "underfoot" and not underfoot, close nearby without being in the way. You can also calm him down if he's excited, or gain immediate control of him if he's in a potentially dangerous situation. Of course the puppy must completely trust you in order to obey this command in a highly emotional situation, such as in a crowd or on a street corner. Work indoors on the down-stay, gradually increasing the length of the exercise.

OFF

Off is the command for those times when your dog is jumping up, no matter if it's on you, your spouse, a neighbor, a stranger, or a dining room chair. Using your voice in a harsh, explosive way will usually convey your displeasure to the puppy. We're suggesting you use the word *off*, though any word in English or Japanese will do the job of startling the puppy. Likely you will have to remove the puppy the first few (hundred) times, physically with your hand on the scruff of his neck, in order for him to understand that you mean business. Once he's down on all fours again, praise him and move on.

An adult Labrador Retriever jumping up is very dangerous. Teach the dog the off command when he is young and weighs less than you do!

OK

A positive command! A command that isn't based on nagging the puppy. Next to dinner or eat, this will be your puppy's favorite word. Your puppy will be happy to hear your voice granting him permission. Introduce the *OK* when you are offering him his bone, his dinner, or opening a door for him to enter or exit. In time the puppy will wait to hear this word as you open a front door or his crate door, before crossing a street at your side, and before greeting a new person, etc.

WAIT

This word is human for wait. Teach it to the puppy the same way you'd teach it to a child—it's recommended that you wait until the puppy is at least six months old before introducing this word. It is practically the same as stay except that the puppy will know that it won't be as lengthy or as intense. The word can be reinforced with a *no*, which will get the puppy's attention. Puppies hear a lot of words, garble that is. They have to recognize when the word is a command and not just more garble that they aren't expected to understand. Much of this garble, we realize, is pleasant for the dog, especially if directed at the puppy in a loving tone of voice. Your voice should change when you speak to the puppy. Concentrate on being clear and distinct, authoritative or cheerful, convincing or calming: the garble takes on meaning, even if every word isn't a known command.

Give your dog something worth waiting for: after the dog has waited, reward him with a new Nylabone® or something else he loves.

ENOUGH

Let's attempt to not overuse the *no* command, lest we nag our dogs and they lose heart. In a word, the *enough* command expresses your disapproval of a dog's continuing to do what he's doing. A dog seems to instinctively grasp this command, mainly because he doesn't have to do anything except look up at you and decide why you're shouting at him. By this time, he's stopped doing whatever it was that annoys you and he's obeyed the command.

HERE

To present food, a new toy, or whatever you are giving your dog, say *here*. The word will capture the dog's attention until you present something.

OUT/DROP IT

When playing ball or Frisbee®, the command can mean let go or release the object. Out can also be an invitation to the dog that he's going in the yard or for a walk.

Say "night" every time your puppy enters his crate. Soon he'll know that it's time to retire in the crate whenever you announce that it's nighttime.

WALK

The wonder word, the "W" word, *walk* can lift a dog's spirits and let him know that a favorite activity is about to happen. He will likely dance around you while you gather his leash and your coat. Don't tease a dog with the "W" word because he'll become frustrated and unhappy. When in conversation with a non-canine friend, you may have to spell this word so that the dog doesn't start two-stepping around the front door.

NIGHT/SLEEP

This tells your dog that it's time to retire for the evening, playtime is over, no more nighttime snacks. On the command, the dog should enter his crate and settle in. Some folks use the word "kennel" instead, but it's too institutional for my home.

BAD Habits and Prevention

Your puppy knows that you are the boss, the pack leader, the provider. He trusts and loves you; he looks to you for guidance, encouragement, the best fun. You are consistent and your puppy knows what's good or bad. Let's not try to teach the puppy every *yes* and *no* from the first day. We must decide which behaviors are the most undesirable and redirect those first. Were we to shout *no* at the puppy every time he ventured into wrongdoing, his first year would be one long nag, and the puppy would begin to look like a disoriented lawn ornament—a schizoid flamingo or cross-eyed jockey.

Training a puppy occurs one day at a time. Don't expect your puppy to be the perfect house pet in the first 24 hours. There will be accidents, messes, and near-disasters...and YOU are always to blame.

It's always a good idea to distract the puppy when he's finding mischief. Call him to you so that he forgets what he's getting into. This is part of problem prevention, though you can't be there 48 hours a day.

A puppy experiences growing pains: teeth are

erupting, sex organs become distracting, personality is blossoming, and the need to test his owner's limits and the boundaries of his

Treat your puppy as the intelligent and sensitive creature he is.

Nothing is as obsessive to the puppy as his mouth suddenly bursting with fangs that feel funny. Give him sensible, safe chew devices (such as a Gumabone®) before he finds devices of his own.

territory become central. Keep these things in mind as you guide your puppy through his ever-changing world. The puppy typically experiences three fear periods, when he needs to test his master. They occur at various ages depending on breed and dog. It's enough to be aware that these tests of will are normal. The puppy's teeth are annoying to him: they erupt at around 16 weeks and again at around 8 months. Teething and chewing problems may be annoying to you but they're obsessive to him. Male puppies especially become territorial and protective, usually around three months of age. They become aggressive, feisty, and barky. All this and then his body starts kicking in, too. The male puppy will be reaching sexual maturity at around 4 months; the female puppy a little later, depending on breed, from 7 to 12 months. Don Juan puppy will begin thrusting his attitude and pelvis on furniture legs and your legs in no time at all. He is intense and intent on saving his species, like all other males in the universe. Normal? You bet. Guinevere puppy will also begin to experience hormonal changes. Female puppies are more dominant than males and will dominate over any males in the household, canine or human. Her hormones are flowering; she becomes more excitable, "bitchier," and may react irrationally, getting mushy during Kodak™ commercials on TV, or worse.

YOUNG AIREDALE TERRIER PUPPY SEEKS SAME FOR ADVENTURE AND SAFE FUN.

All of these puppy statistics and generalizations have an affect on the puppy's trainability and ability to concentrate, and explain some of the sources of the bad habits that you as the master need to eradicate.

CRYING

Young puppies may act like babies in more than one way. Crying through the night and not giving their "parents" any rest is a prime example. Fortunately, puppies usually outgrow this stage faster than their human counterparts. Lullabies and rocking, however, aren't the cure-alls here. We keep in mind that the puppy is insecure and not accustomed to spending the night by his lonesome. His mother and siblings are no longer around for warmth and comfort. He is now alone in a dog crate, which we know simulates a den experience for him, but he may not be grasping that concept on the first night.

The old wives' tale of a ticking clock and a hot water bottle is still often told, though its credibility is limited. How dopey do we think a dog can be?! Smart, inquiring puppies will unwrap the clock (to find out what's ticking) and chew on the water bottle (to see if it responds like their former puppy playmates or mama's breast). Obviously these items aren't puppy-proof, and you may find yourself running to the vet to remove the rubber particles and wind-up key from your wet puppy's belly.

Holding an excited puppy in this fashion may serve to quiet him down. Be reassuring and brief if you need to console a traumatized first-nighter. The pup needs only to know that you're still close by.

You should never scold a puppy for crying during the night, nor should you consider punishment. Punishment reinforces a puppy's fear and diminishes his trust in you. At this vital time, you are trying to convince the puppy that you're the next best thing since beef jerky: you need

him to trust you. Comfort the puppy with sweet talk, using his name and perhaps a single dog treat. Do not give him a handful lest he'll have an accident during the night. Scratch his

"First night in the new crate without your mom— you'd whine too!" Forlorn Bichon Frise youngster trying to grasp a new concept: "A den, you say?"

head through the crate. Turn on the radio: sweet sounds and mellow human voices will ease his discomfort. These difficult nights do not persist typically. Be gentle and kind, understanding that everything is new and exciting to the puppy, and scary too. If the crying does go on for more than a week to ten days, you should have the puppy reexamined by your veterinarian to check for any possible problems.

NIPPING

Young puppies are very oral. As with all mammals, life begins with sucking. Once the teeth begin to erupt, the puppy needs to feel them, to test them, to sharpen them. Your job as master is to make it clear to the puppy immediately that the bones in your hands and arms are not made of nylon!

Human bones aren't made of nylon, so it's wise to keep your limbs out of the growing Rottweiler's jaws. A Nylabone® serves the purpose far better.

Gnawing on human bones is not acceptable, even if they taste better than nylon or polyurethane.

The *no* command will do wonders with the puppy. When you're playing with the puppy and he begins mouthing you, say *no*. Do not grab his mouth and hold it shut. This makes the puppy crazy— he'll forget where he is and what he was doing and only concentrate on escaping your grasp on his most important of all body parts. (Mind you, this is a prepubescent puppy!) You may have to remove him by the scruff of the neck or gently shake him if he doesn't respond to your *no*. We must mean business when we correct the puppy from nipping. Remember those little

Not every dog is as civilized as these two furry beauties from Orientals O'BJ. Bill and BJ Andrews pose with a Chinese Foo Dog and one of the great O'BJ Akitas.

sharp milkteeth, which merely pinch now, will eventually erupt into strong canines and incisors developed by God to rip meat from bones. Regardless of your puppy's breed, any dog's teeth can do damage to an adult, no less a child who is the puppy's playmate.

The crate is a sensible mode of correction for nipping. The puppy will quickly understand that if he doesn't play by your rules, he's playing by himself. Putting the puppy in his crate will make the puppy feel duly ignored. Puppies hate to be ignored, as do children.

The other reason that God didn't make humans' bones nylon is so that we could have Nylabones® for our puppies. These bones are another answer to the nipping puppy. We know that he's nipping to exercise his incoming chompers, to playfully assert his dominance, to play. We can redirect all those intentions with a Nylabone®. Introduce the Nylabone® during a play session. Your puppy will

Two Bulldog puppies making a wish....for clean teeth and strong jaws. The Gumabone® Wishbone™ tastefully obliges.

be thrilled to have new things to sink his teeth into. The Nylabone Corporation has spent decades and millions of dollars developing effective chew devices for dogs of all ages, sizes and breeds. If the traditional Nylabone is too hard for the puppy, there are Gumabones®, Chicken Nylabones®, and many others, in all sizes. Give him the bone when he starts to gnaw on you, tap it, play with it, lick it if you have to, leave it with him in the crate—he's sure to figure it out.

CHEWING

Like nipping, chewing relates to the puppy's need to exercise his developing teeth, to massage his gums, to work on his jaw. Chewing is vital to dogs. It does not need to be eliminated, simply redirected. Chewing is

The alternative to a Nylabone® may be your favorite tennis shoes....they smell almost as good but don't last nearly as long.

Destructive chewing habits can be prevented. Puppies will chew on anything that doesn't chew back.

really much like tennis, a good book or movie, a visit to the masseur or therapist, a happy-hour cocktail—all ways to relieve tensions! Since dogs don't read or drink socially and can't get country club memberships (at least not in America), they opt to chew! Redirecting the chewing desire brings us back to Nylabones®, safe effective chew devices. You can correct the dog when he's chewing on the linoleum or floorboards with a stern *no*, and then say *OK* and give him a Nylabone®. It is not advisable to toss him an old sneaker or boot, since he won't be able to differentiate between those discarded items and your new Nikes™ or Bostonians™. Many trainers recommend spraying such objects with Bitter Apple™ or rubbing alcohol to make them undesirable. Don't overdue these sprays as they can be harmful if ingested in large amounts. (Read the labels.) Take him over to the undesirable object and let him taste it. He should react negatively. Some dogs may not react to this at all. Another possibility is to scold the object that the puppy is chewing, say *no*, and smack the floorboard or shoe. Be sure the neighbors aren't watching.

Most dogs cannot sing, though this one can. The New Guinea Singing Dog vocalizes like no other mammal (other than the humpback whale) and instinctively harmonizes with its pack mates. Photograph courtesy of Janice A. Koler.

For the safety of the animal, be sure to remove any harmful wires, objects, etc., from the puppy's area. Puppyproofing has much to do with what the puppy can and will put in his mouth. Remember puppies are curious and, above all, oral.

BARKING

Imagine for a moment that dogs didn't bark. Instead they talked. In our own language. Sure, some of the difficulties of communication would be eliminated sooner, but consider the unending, ubiquitous list of wants and groans we'd have to live with. Dogs are naturally greedy animals—sharing is not part of the canine mindset. Crates wouldn't be too blissful if we had to listen to our puppy's interminable complaining from within. We'd wish they were just whining. Puppies are to be seen and not heard. And what if they could sing? "The doggy in *what* window?"

Barking, like chewing, is perfectly normal. Since dogs *don't* talk, and we can be grateful for that small miracle,

Not all barking is bad. Decide when a dog's barking is constructive and reward him. Give him outlets to show off his voice so that he doesn't abuse his vocal gifts.

they bark, whine, and howl in order to communicate. Our first consideration with solving problem barking is to determine which barking is problematic. We are principally concerned with excessive barking, barking at the air, a moth, a mother-in-law, or some other unavoidable presence. Territorial barking isn't necessarily an evil. If your breed is a guard dog or a viable watchdog, barking can be a blessing as it can signal an invasion of your property. Thus barking is part of the reason for owning such a dog. Granted, a Chihuahua or Lhasa Apso barking ferociously at the mailman is not the same thing. Dogs also bark to show dominance, as they would have in the wild within their pack order. Barking at people, in general, is undesirable and may be a precursor to biting.

Over the years, training manuals have forced into print some of the most unbelievable methods of curbing barking. We're not saying that some of those methods didn't work on some dog somewhere, but their general acceptance is dubious at best. Whether your dog will react to a bucket of water mysteriously hurled on him when he barks outdoors I can't predict. Nor can I tell you whether he'll quickly quiet when a flying sheet or scarecrow topples over your picket fence.

Training starts at home, which is to say, indoors. If the puppy is barking unnecessarily, use the shaker can. He may associate barking with this undesirable sound and bark less. Teach him to speak on command. This may give him an outlet to exercise his beautiful voice.

On the occasion that you need to stop his barking, tell him that he's done good as you quiet him. Perhaps he's

alerted you to a person at the front door or to a raccoon in the garbage cans, or it may just be the usual nine o'clock cat fight or his own shadow on the windowpane. Thank him and say good-bye. Don't make the outburst an event.

The hound breeds were bred for their bellows! The Bloodhound, the true *basso profundos of the dog world, has a thunderous bark that (you hope) he uses with great discretion.*

Never leave a puppy outdoors during the day. This is not only unsafe but can help to develop the habitual barker. Never encourage the puppy to speak for his dinner or to go out.

Keep in mind that certain breeds and kinds of dogs have been trained to use their voices for work. Therefore, if you have a Basset Hound, Beagle, Coonhound, or another scenthound breed that has been raised to "give voice" on a trail or in a pack, your commitment to the barking problem needs to be more devoted. Did you know the Finnish Spitz is prized for

A quiet Finnish Spitz is uncharacteristic of the Barking Dog of Finland. Finskis bark in unique patterns with definite dynamics and pitch control.

his voice in his native Finland and in his homeland is judged on the basis of bark in the show ring? The mastiff breeds with strong protective instincts will also be more vocal than other breeds, such as the Chow Chow and Shiba Inu, who give voice more discriminately. Of course, the Basenji doesn't bark at all, but he does yodel, which is a little better than singing!

Two Basenji puppies on their way to yodeling class.

Finally, remember that puppies bark for a reason, just like babies cry for a reason. Your puppy may be anxious, upset, hungry, or uncomfortable. Dogs have a sixth sense about their environment, or simply have better ears than we do. Consider if there is something bothering him. Remove the stimulus and you'll eliminate that barking. Be sensitive to your dog's needs. He may be hearing animals outside or other night noises that are unfamiliar and unsettling. Or maybe he's just talkative. One barky night doesn't guarantee a habitual problem.

Evening may find your puppy active and alert, especially if he has been alone for much of the day.

Puppies learn what is acceptable in play from their dams and siblings. Owners need to establish the ground rules from the very beginning so that the rambunctious six-week-old understands the law.

JUMPING UP

In the wild, young wolf pups greet their elders by jumping up and licking their muzzles. This greeting indicates a friendly hello or that the puppies are hungry. Puppies also play by jumping up on one another, wrestling, and nipping at each other. They learn the ropes and what is acceptable and still fun from their siblings. Puppies, therefore, need to learn boundaries from their human keepers.

Teaching the puppy not to jump up is simple if you are consistent. It must begin when the puppy is young, even if the hello greetings are adorable and harmless. A 75-pound adult dog bounding for you when your arms are full of groceries is neither adorable nor harmless. Start when the puppy is young. Tell him *off* when he jumps

How cute is a puppy on his hind legs begging for food or attention? In four months, this adorable Dalmatian puppy will be able to knock down an adult with just as little effort.

up. Place him on the floor by using his collar and tell him *sit*. Praise while he's on the floor. He will learn that he can only greet you from all fours. Lean down and give him a hug and a kiss. Some dogs will greet you with a little two-step on his twos. This is wonderful as long as he returns to all fours once you approach him. Always give him his kisses once he's back on the floor. Owners of small breeds do not have as big a concern with this as large-breed owners, for obvious reasons. The Shiba owner is delighted by his miniatures' dancing upon his homecoming; the Akita owner is afraid. Keep in mind that your guests may not be as delighted by the dog's greeting as you are, or that you may not want the dog jumping up on you when you're all dolled up with ribbons down your back. Teach him to not jump up anyway. It's simply better and safer. Once he's trained, you can always *invite* the dog to greet you on his twos once in a while.

If a simple *no* doesn't keep the dog from jumping up, you can avoid the dog's jumping up by lifting your knee so that the dog hits his chest into your knee. Another safe method is to clasp your hands in front of you so that he hits his nose. The dog will not want to jump up on you whenever he see you with your knee up or your hands clasped. Repeat this method every time the dog jumps up. Do not try to practice this correction by creating a jumping-up situation. This can make the dog think that this is a game. The creative dog will try to find ways of dodging your knee or hands, or start nipping or jumping higher.

Teach your puppy that the only *place to ever find food is in his bowl and you'll never have to deal with a beggar at dinner.*

BEGGING

Begging is annoying, so, at risk of being politically incorrect, don't give in to a beggar. Needy puppies aren't attractive. Yes, a begging puppy can be irresistible. Avoid the puppy's begging by never feeding him from the dinner table. This is not to say that a hand treat is a bad thing, nor is it to say that table scraps are bad. Good table scraps are good. Feed the puppy after you have eaten dinner. Occasionally add table scraps to his food. Dogs are omnivores, not carnivores; they eat meat and vegetables and table scraps can perk up an ordinary dinner. You shouldn't do this every night or else the puppy will become fussy. Do not feed the puppy before you eat your dinner. You're the master, you eat first. Keep in mind that you do not want to interrupt your housetraining schedule. If you feed the puppy first, he may not be interested in his food, knowing that your better-smelling victuals will follow soon. If you are already guilty of feeding the puppy from the table, stop immediately. If he continues to beg, you may have to remove him from the dinner area. Crate him or put him in a sit-stay or down-stay.

JUMPING ON FURNITURE

Prevention, as always, is the easiest cure. Do not allow your puppy on furniture; keep him away from the furniture; get rid of all your sofas and chairs so that the puppy can have free rein of the living room without jumping on the furniture.

Since these options aren't too viable, we'll have to come up with a plan of action to keep the puppy from jumping up. Be consistent. Don't let the puppy sit on the couch in the evening and then scold him during the daytime for the very same behavior. Ideally your puppy likes you and wants to be near you. Some breeds are more snugglesome than others. Some puppies may

A Kodak™ moment: Dalmatian puppy sleeping under a handmade blanket on the living room sofa. Remember you can't photograph first and scold second. Be consistent and decide what's acceptable from the start.

If your correction turns into a game, you have failed. Regardless of how unexpectedly cute the puppy's next move is, you must concentrate on making him understand your intentions.

need to be curled up at your feet on the couch; other puppies just want to be sitting across the room from you.

This behavior can be modified by allowing the puppy into your living area wearing his leash. Remove him from the furniture with his leash, tell him *off*. On the second offense, put him in a down-stay or sit-stay. Another feasible method is to use the shaker can in association with the *no* correction. This is just one further use for the shaker can.

The puppy simply cannot be trusted to have the run of the house before he is *completely* housetrained. Therefore there is no real way to keep him off the furniture. He's not happy that you're not home. The living room furniture smells like you, as does your bed, slippers and hairbrush. He wants to be near you, so when you're not home he's bound to be sitting on your furniture, napping on your bed, or snacking on your slippers.

There are probably a number of methods that would work in isolated cases, but the only sure way I know to keep the dog off the furniture until he knows better and is completely trained is to keep him in his crate or at least puppy-gated in a different room.

Almost doesn't count in housebreaking. If the puppy isn't completely dependable in the house, he should not be granted license to every room.

RUNNING WILD

A puppy let out into the main living area of the home on occasion may tear about the house wildly. This is reckless and dangerous, usually referred

to as the "crazies." Crazies are preventable, to an extent. If your puppy has been crated for a long while, let him run outdoors or take him for a brisk walk on his leash. The crazies occur because the dog's energy tank is on "F" and he needs to burn some of his puppy petrol. It is best to introduce the puppy to the other areas of the house after he has exercised and relieved himself. Another bad side of the crazies is that, after a vigorous run, the excitement, and being confined for a while, the puppy will need to relieve himself immediately. Never let him run in the house unsupervised. A puppy who is not fully housebroken should be confined to a room or his crate for his own safety and not given the entire house to ransack.

Labrador puppies invented the "crazies." Most sporting breed puppies are untiring, able to run and play for hours on end.

AGGRESSION

The bully, macho puppy likely does not have a problem with aggression. The shy or fearful puppy that growls or even nips does not have an aggression problem either. The spoiled dog or the dog trained by the lenient master, or the master who hasn't read a single training manual and lets the puppy get away with hell and high-water, does not have an aggression problem.

Puppies grow out of these undesirable habits. However, the puppy that growls at you or your children while being fed, walked, petted or brushed does have an aggression problem. You, as the alpha and master, must take on this aggressive problem by the ears, or scruff, as it were. This puppy needs to be reminded that he is not the leader in the household. You need to scold him confidently whenever he growls—don't sweet talk him into being nice. He'll misinterpret your loving tones to say, "You like that big bark, don't you?" A growling puppy can lead to far worse as he grows up. If necessary, shake him by the scruff of the neck and say *no* in a stern voice. Only for the worst of surly offenders should you attempt to dominant-down the dog (rolling him on his back and holding him down). While the dominant-down is a serious correction and is not recommended for frequent use, it is better than allowing a puppy to develop into an unmanageable tyrant, or worse.

Although there are many breeds of dog that are

This gang of butch bulldogs is working on a ferocious stance.

Staffordshire Terriers make excellent family dogs, as protective and imposing as they are sweet and obedient. No dog can outclass a properly trained Staff.

naturally aggressive, no breed of dog should be aggressive toward people, only other dogs. Admittedly there are certain mastiff breeds that were originally used to track down humans, and these dogs, if improperly socialized, can be problematic. The Bullmastiff, Argentine Dogo and Neapolitan Mastiff serve as examples of such guard dogs. The bull and terrier breeds, such as the American Pit Bull Terrier, American Staffordshire Terrier, Staffordshire Bull Terrier, and Bull Terrier, can be naturally aggressive toward one another as a result of their fighting-dog backgrounds. These breeds today, in the right loving hands, present few problems as non-aggressive companion animals. Other breeds, such as the Akita, Rottweiler, Doberman Pinscher, and Komondor, can be unmanageable and aggressive if not properly reared and trained.

Any dog—whether one of the purebreds above, a smaller, amiable toy dog, or an innocent crossbreed—can be genetically programmed to be aggressive. You cannot predict this predisposition. Though it is helpful to have

What makes an aggressive dog? Observe the behavior of canines at play and you'll see that much of their roughhousing and fighting consist mostly of posturing and ritual.

visited the parents of your puppy to observe their dispositions, this does not clear your puppy of the possibility of having had a trigger-happy uncle somewhere down the line. Some dogs are overly sensitive, vulnerable, insecure, or afraid, and compensate by becoming aggressive. If the puppy has had little groundwork in training, his fear period—the

Make eye contact with the puppy to indicate to him that you're the top dog. Alpha puppies will avoid eye contact and squirm when forced to look you in the eye.

Rottweilers possess strong protective instincts and can be trained to bring down a man. These puppies and dam are playing with a Schutzhund guardwork sleeve. Training for such work must be undertaken with extreme care.

period where a dog naturally tests his owner and his limits— may be more intense.

These incurable alpha types will mark around your house, sleep where they wish, jump up when they hear a can opener, not allow you to go near them while they're

eating, and bully your kids around. The dog has adopted near-terrorist tactics to assert his dominance; such hostility to become the alpha figure must be met with immediate attention. We recognize this dog's body language instantly: his mouth and lips are snarling; his teeth are showing; his ears and hackles are raised; his body is arched and his tail is directly up. The worst-case scenario involves the dog actually biting you, your children, or visitors. A biting dog is a risky situation and not one to be taken lightly.

Although it is the scorpion's nature to sting, it is not the dog's nature to bite. Nevertheless, a problem biter is not an unheard-of phenomenon in the dog world.

If the dog refuses to heed your commands, you must get tougher on him or else his transgressions will only multiply. In the process of training, you must not tolerate any aggressive signs. Do not comfort a dog who is filing his incisors on your leg bone. This

Dogs do not bite humans by nature. Treated kindly from puppyhood and with proper socialization, any dog can become a trustworthy, loving companion.

will reassure him that it's okay to chew on mommy and that you're perfectly content with his pearly whites ripping through your new Calvin Kleins™. Only praise the dog when he's doing right; praise and condolence shouldn't be substituted. Praise is important, as is correction; don't get so caught up in predicting his next wrong move that you forget to praise him at the appropriate times.

The Pug derived from mastiff breeds with strong, aggressive instincts. Inside every Pug is the heart of a 200-pound brute waiting to escape.

It is wise to not use food rewards when training a dog that is naturally aggressive. Positive reinforcement will help keep your tank of a tyke in his proper place in the pack. Food goes to the alpha dog first. Likewise don't attempt to eat a sandwich while teaching your dog to sit-stay or else he'll lose his concentration and you'll lose your tuna. In training an aggressive dog, be sure to be very hands-on. He must get accustomed to people touching him, and this helps to nurture the bond between you, his master and trainer, and the dog.

When dealing with a large breed like the Rottweiler, take no chances: seek professional assistance if the dog becomes unruly or isn't responding to your corrections.

If the dog isn't responding to firm leash corrections and your commands of *no*; or if he's nipping, you will need to seek a professional's assistance. While you may be able to live with a dog that barks twice too often or insists on snoozing on your ottoman, you cannot live with a dog that bites. Your decision to deal with a problem dog like this one does not make you less of a person, or a bad dog person. You are being a responsible member of society, since aggressive dogs do not benefit anyone.

DIGGING

Dogs dig. Mama Nature gave them the paws and the cause, and so dogs dig to uncover food, to find water, shade, shelter, or last year's ripe stew bone. Why is your puppy digging? If he's hot in an open yard, it may be for shade. Then he's telling you something—he's trying to cool himself down. If he's neither hot, thirsty nor unsheltered, he may be engaging in recreational digging.

The excitement of homecoming. Kuro and breeder Rick Tomita.

The puppy is bored, and digging is fun, especially in the soft ground around your tulips or under the porch where it's "air conditioned." Many experts recommend allowing the dog to dig in one area only—you bring the pup there whenever he's redesigning your landscape. Another option is to occupy the puppy whenever he starts to dig. Give him a new Nylabone®, take him for a brisk walk, or engage in a game of fetch—anything to distract him from the good earth. Not every digging problem can be covered up—various methods have worked for some trainers, but there are no absolutes. You may just have a real diggety dog: the terriers are notoriously talented diggers, though hounds and huskies can burrow with the best of them.

WETTING

Not to be confused with a housebreaking problem, the puppy wets when he's excited or threatened. Never scold the piddling offender! It's best to ignore the puppy after such an incident. You should learn to recognize the signs of fear and excitement in the puppy and try to soothe the puppy. Some trainers attempt to teach these puppies to urinate on command so that you can assure that the pup's bladder is empty before he greets you indoors. You can also offer a food treat so that the puppy knows he's good and shouldn't be afraid. Be patient, praise and reassure the puppy, and soon the problem will eliminate itself, so to speak. (You may want to check with your veterinarian to see if there is a physical problem that can be treated.)

SMARTER Than Your Average Pup

What is your puppy thinking when he looks up at you adoringly? Is he thinking? Really thinking? This question has smarted the greatest thinkers mankind has known: Aristotle, Descartes, Shakespeare, Darwin, and St. Thomas Aquinas....not to mention Dave Barry and Gary Larson. Aristotle, perhaps the greatest of these, believed that dogs could indeed think, just not to the same degree as man could.

How smart is your puppy? The perfect student: an alert Border Collie puppy ready to take on the world and herd everyone into a happier corral.

We know today that dogs do something that looks like thinking: they learn from mistakes, solve problems, and gain from their experiences. We do not clump the dog in with lower primates but consider his abilities to be closer to higher forms of life, like gorillas, chimpanzees, and dolphins.

These Labrador puppies learn by seeing and doing. Spend time with your puppy and keep his mind and paws active. Few breeds can learn as much and as readily as the Labrador Retriever.

The American Bulldog shines as the next up-and-coming "I-can-do-anything" purebred. These talented and attractive dogs excel in every area in which they are trained.

Clearly the dog, like these other mammals, does not benefit from linguistics as does man: no other mammal is capable of speech, though all of them still actively communicate with one another, without language barriers or generation gaps. Actually, although the dogs in America say woof-woof and the dogs of France say *oua-oua,* they still understand each other far better than any American or Frenchman possibly could.

Since dogs have not become caught up in human emotions, societal expectations, and the like, they remain more instinctual. Humans, on the other hand, think instead of act. Dogs can follow their impulses, senses, and instincts with few, if any, worries and less expectations.

We expect dogs to put on human faces and emotions. A recent attack of two pit bull terriers on an elderly couple was reported through the national news. The accounts condemned the dogs retained in the pound, describing them as "appearing uncaring." Dogs do not rationalize; they do not feel guilt; they do not premeditate; they do not perceive wrong in the human philosophical sense. But they do think.

The author's two Shiba Inu, Kabuki and Tengu, suffer from selective-hearing disorder. They oddly enough always hear the words "walk" and "eat" (their two favorite activities).

Have you ever pondered what your dog is thinking when he runs from one room to another in search of a favorite toy? Why does he run to get his cherry-red Gumabone®, not his new rawhide or his ball, but the red bone? The idea had to enter his head and he had to execute the thought. Compared to the tasks of obedience trial dogs, this one is a wee accomplishment.

As the owner of one of the most difficult breeds of dogs to train, I can assure you that only a thinking animal can possess selective hearing. Both my Shiba Inu have this charming and aggravating quality. Selective hearing means, of course, they hear only what they choose to hear....suddenly the animal goes completely deaf and stares off in another direction, pondering the universe and its many fascinating components.

We know dogs are social animals, and as social animals they have a real need to communicate with each other and with their human masters and friends. Dogs do try to relay their feelings: their wagging tails tell us they are happy and excited to see us; their teeth bared express their anger; their exposed bellies reveal their complete submission. The dog's gestures and postures are governed by ritual. Any dog recognizes a play bow from another dog, whether he's a giant Mastiff or a tiny Italian Greyhound. Humans can even participate in canine gestures and dogs will accept us playfully. While the dog doesn't recognize you as a dog, he will respond to your posturing and have fun with you. Don't misunderstand and think you can bark and wag your "tail" and have your dog interpret these as anything but play. Only dogs can truly communicate in doggie terms.

Of course, dogs use their voices extensively too. The dog's bark conveys his emotion, it does not necessarily relay information. His sounds are many and meaningful: barking to show us or call us; growling to warn us; whimpering to tell us he's hurt; baying to remind us he's a pack animal; howling to define his territory; yelping to say notice me; sighing ... to sigh. There are many variations of each sound with a pocket dictionary of meanings. We should listen more closely to our dogs, just as we expect them to heed our every word.

While we know that dogs cannot form their own words, we know that they can comprehend many of our words. The average well-trained dog knows 50 to 100

This is dog talk for "Ooh, Aah, Ooooooh!"

words, varying from the obvious sit and stay, to words like jump, kitchen, find, pee, and quiet. Dogs learn words from context as well as from our tone of voice. Dogs respond to how we say words and are sensitive to the rhythm of our language. Just as a dog barks in a series of utterances, or howls or yelps, so do our words become a series of sounds that relay

The play bow is an invitation to play: bow wow wow!

meaning. While we train a puppy using simple one-word commands (plus his name, in certain cases), we have no doubt that a dog can comprehend the gist of a long sentence and even respond to it. Dogs likely think we use too many very superfluous words. For their sake, I won't elaborate....further.

Rottweilers like books written about them, preferably short, fun books read aloud by adoring youngsters.

DISTINCT INSTINCT

To determine dog intelligence, we must rely on generalizations of breed, personality types, and in some cases, the sex of the animal. The most intelligent of all dogs may be the Border Collie, a dog that is highly trainable and only happy when obeying a command. The Border Collie excels in formal obedience trials and complicated sheepdog trials. Herding dogs, developed to follow man's word and hand signals, rank high among the canine brain pack. Among the highest are the German Shepherd Dog, Shetland Sheepdog, and Australian Cattle Dog.

The Border Collie watching over his woolly charges. These Scottish-bred shepherds are capable of learning hundreds of commands (verbal, whistle and hand signals).

The Poodle, too, has long been revered for its higher intelligence among dogs. Theories of the Poodle's large skull size accommodating more brain room were long accepted, though they don't explain the lesser intelligence of other large-headed canines like the English Bulldog, Bullmastiff, or Dogue de Bordeaux. (This latter French mastiff is not terribly smart but does have the largest skull in the dog world.) Nonetheless, the Poodle has excelled in all types of competition and is a favorite of trainers around the world for its quickness of learning and ability to remember. I think

Never at the head of the class, the Dogue de Bordeaux boasts the largest skull in dogdom.

the Poodle is actually smarter than the Border Collie simply because the Poodle doesn't spend long hot days running sheep up and down hills.

Much controversy exists about the intelligence of the Golden Retriever. This delightfully bright dog lives to please his master. He does not excel in field trials to the same extent as the Labrador Retriever. Perhaps the Golden Retriever falters in intense competition because he's a worrier. Labradors work more mechanically and therefore excel in the rigid expectations of a field trial. Statistics will show us that the black male Labrador Retriever is by far the most intelligent of breed members. About 90 percent of all field trial champions have been black male Labrador Retrievers. Females prove more difficult to train than males, and males can stand more rigorous training and are not interrupted by estrus. Both of these working gundogs, the Labrador and Golden, are revered for their smarts. The spaniels and

It's in the genes: black Labrador Retrievers have no competition dominating field trials. They can be trained rigorously and perform flawlessly under environmental and emotional stress.

retrievers in general are regarded as enjoying superior trainability, as is the tiny Papillon, a miniaturized gundog, who is a charm to train.

Doberman Pinschers and Rottweilers, two massive mastiff breeds, have much going for them in the smarts category: brains and brawn in some appealing black and tan packages. Both of these athletic scholars make excellent guard dogs, Schutzhund contenders and obedience trial champions.

While the terrier breeds are typically not recommended for obedience work, the Miniature Schnauzer defies the odds and proves to be among the brightest and most trainable of all dogs. In general, terriers are very single-minded and persistent. It

The Papillon, a miniature spaniel, can go head to head with any dog. Bright and super-alert, Papillons make faithful companions and delightful students.

certainly requires a feisty, fearless dog to burrow into the earth to assail a sharp-toothed half-crazed varmint. Once in the earth, the terrier dog doesn't need a lot of instructions: it is every terrier for himself; this is survival, not silly hand signals and tooting whistles. Most of us forgive our terriers for their inability to breeze through Obedience 101.

The Miniature Schnauzer outshines his terrier brethren in the smarts category. This Mini executes the bar jump at an agility trial.

Those breeds that have been utilized for various tasks, such as the Brittany, Bernese Mountain Dog, Vizsla, Airedale Terrier, and Giant Schnauzer, prove to be more trainable and intelligent. The Vizsla, for example, is among the most versatile of the all-purpose gundogs; the Airedale can perform numerous tasks from terrier, to guard dog, to messenger dog, to obedience dog. These breeds' long histories as helpmates and Renaissance Dogs have led to their high trainability.

Bully for us! Bull and terrier dogs (such as this cartful) thrive on their desire to please humans. Bulldogs can be trained to do anything and always perform with macho gusto.

The hounds prove to be among the more difficult breeds to train. The Beagle, a small scent hound, is infamous for his potty-training slowness; as a matter of fact, Beagles and most of the scenthound breeds (Foxhounds, Bassets, Coonhounds) are slow learners. These dogs were not bred and selected for trainability as much as for their noses and gregariousness as pack animals. Their transition from outdoor pack animals to indoor pets proves difficult. Housetraining is not part of outdoor life. Similarly, the sighthound breeds (Greyhound, Saluki, Whippet, Afghan Hound) are not quick learners either. This is attributed more to their independent mindset and limited motivation to please

Beagles tend to be slow learners—unless there's food involved. This handsome fellow not only can open the refrigerator but he is also adept at fixing midnight snacks.

Philosophical and peke-faced, this Oriental doll rarely finds time for commands. Pekingese prefer quiet contemplation.

their masters. As superior, self-sufficient hunters, these dogs traditionally had little to depend on man for and didn't place much confidence in man's stewardship. The Northern breeds, such as the Siberian Husky and Alaskan Malamute, also don't confide in man as readily as most other types of dogs. These dogs were bred to pull sleds: they depended on the pack pecking system where one dog was "king." Of course no sled dog worth his salt looks behind him once in the hitch—it's all forward moving and forward thinking. Another noteworthy similarity between the sighthounds and the Northern breeds is the futility of considering off-leash training. Though for different reasons, neither the greyhound dogs nor the huskies should be worked in an off-leash manner. The sighthounds aren't called "dogs of the wind" for nothing—they're off and running in an instant. Oddly this same flight instinct is ever-present in the huskies or spitzen as well, who are also excellent runners. The Shiba Inu cannot be trusted without his leash—small and fleetfooted, this trouble-making wonder will be halfway to Japan before the golden sun sets.

Among the least trainable of dogs are dogs of Eastern descent, certainly not a reflection of the industrious East today but more related to the personality and aloofness of these dogs. They prove to distract easily (or intentionally), bore quickly, and insist on independent thinking. Among the Eastern free-thinkers are the Shih Tzu, Lhasa Apso, Pekingese, Chow Chow, and Tibetan Terrier, to insinuate a few. Are these dogs unintelligent because they are less trainable? Certainly not. This aloofness is typically attributed to cats.

The definition of aloof, the Afghan Hound has stumped more trainers than any other dog. Free running and free thinking, the sighthounds cannot be tethered (but must be leashed).

The willingness of a dog to respond to a command can improve or completely destroy his trainability. It is likely that the Chow Chow or Peke. understands what is asked of him immediately, maybe as quickly as a Border Collie or Poodle, but he has no apparent desire to please his master. In order to train these Eastern-type dogs, they must be socialized carefully to increase their desire to please.

Ever popular and trainable, Poodles need owners who can challenge them and direct them or else they can become yappy pillow-sitters.

As keepers and trainers of dogs, we realize how pertinent a dog's background is to his trainability, intelligence, and motivational drives. No two dogs are equal, whether the same breed, different breeds, or mixed breeds. We can appreciate each dog *as an individual*, loving him for his uniqueness, his brightness, or his independence. Every dog is a new challenge. Whether we are blessed with a Border Collie who can apply physics and calculus or burdened with a flunkie Poodle who would rather be at the beauty salon, we must be well prepared for the challenge of molding our canine charge into a fine and worthy companion.

German Shepherd puppies possess the desire and ability to achieve great things. This Future Leader Dog has been selected to become a guide dog for the blind.

Here's a winning Poodle who can do it all, participating in a flyball competition at Camp Gone to the Dogs. Photograph courtesy of Charlotte Schwartz, author of Training Your Dog for Sports.

EVERY-DAY Things for Your Puppy

L et's talk about a couple ordinary topics, things that we humans do daily and dogs don't: driving and bathing. Some dogs love both, some dogs hate both. We're aiming to have our puppy join the first team. Motoring America's highways with a happy, squeaky clean, well-groomed dog peering out the window of a new Mercedes is the wish of every human being.

THE PUPPY AND THE AUTOMOBILE

Unless your breeder lives next door or down the block, your puppy by now has already been in an automobile. And since all breeders advise to take the puppy to the veterinarian immediately after purchase, maybe he's even been in a car twice by now. Unless, of course, your veterinarian lives next door too! Then you are a lucky individual, and so is your puppy.

For the rest of you poor unfortunate souls who don't live next door to your breeder and veterinarian, you will need to get your puppies accustomed to riding in a car. Some dogs absolutely adore driving in the car: seeing the sights, whizzing by dogs being walked and the lights and the faces, and sniffing the bus fumes. Other dogs go absolutely berserk!—scampering about the backseat, shaking and barking, climbing onto the driver's lap, and humping the gearshift. Not a pretty picture *(photo not available)*.

The truth is that the only absolutely safe way for a dog to travel in a car is in his crate. Unfortunately, most dog people think this takes the fun out of a Sunday drive—and that a portable crate can be a real hassle. It's easier to let 'ol Marbles jump in the back seat and off we go. (Marbles, as you may not know, is a rescue dog that we found and somebody else lost—that's why we call him Marbles.) The completely untrained Marbles bounces all over the backseat, marks the new seat covers, and whines uncontrollably to and from the veterinarian.

When introducing a puppy to a car, do it on a day that you're not going anywhere. Especially not to the veterinarian's office! Be sure the puppy has piddled and has not drank water for a couple hours. Sit in the car with the dog on his leash. Let him get comfortable, leave the door open, give him a tidbit, turn on the radio, read a book (something short, like this book— *Bonfire of the Vanities* will kill your battery).

Driving permit in hand, this adolescent Poodle is ready for the highway.

Decide whether you will use the crate or perhaps a doggy harness, which is pretty handy and makes your puppy look like Laika, the first dog in space. Adorable. He may not even hate it. Perhaps acclimate him to the harness in the house, even before sitting in the car with your book.

The next time you attempt this feat, you will sit in the car, turn on the radio, and then turn the engine over. If you're the kind of person who is training the puppy as a full-time job, that's enough for lesson two. If you're normal like the rest of those reading this book, you don't really have 15 days to acclimate the little bugger to the 10-minute drive to the vet, and you'll actually drive this time. Of course, if your dog really does not like his visits to your parked car, don't rush the process. It's difficult to undo a car-scared puppy.

Whether it's lesson two or lesson three, we're going to drive around the neighborhood. Show your new friend the sites; point to his favorite trees; make "raspberries" at the Beagle he hates as you pass; have a ball. DON'T DRIVE TO THE VET'S! This is his first ride, a joy ride.

If the puppy associates the car with an unhappy ending, he'll not want to get in the car. Your puppy prefers happy endings! So take him to a musical...and bring a friend! If you pay for your friend's ticket, he'll probably help calm the dog in the car. Seriously, two people in the car is the better way to a calm puppy and a safe drive.

These little trips are good socialization time for the puppy as well. Talk to the puppy and reassure him. Praise him for not panicking. Some dogs have a real problem with noise-making in the car, a.k.a. barking, whining, wheezing. If you're the driver, you will have difficulty making any convincing correction to the dog, who is obviously all worked up by the movie that's being shown from every window. Maybe they're bad guys he sees. Maybe he knows he's not at a musical and that there's no happy ending.

Puppy's first experience in a travel crate should be pleasant and fun. Hanging out with a Cocker buddy can take the edge off confinement.

Wire crates give the dog more ventilation and freedom to look around. Most dominant breeds of dog prefer this type crate. Wire crates are not acceptable for air or rail travel.

Tell the barking dog *enough* or another comparable polite word to quiet down. Likely he will quiet down before long. If he's simply too excited in the car, you may have no choice but that un-fun crate.

Although most dogs love the chance to take a drive, some puppies, and even older dogs, never get used to riding in the car. Carsickness can occur in a dog who cannot remain balanced while in a moving vehicle. This is most unpleasant for the dog and no fun for the driver, who's swerving through rush hour while the very nauseous Marbles is drooling and heaving on his lap. You should be aware of signs of the forthcoming carsickness before the scenario gets this bad. Go slowly through the acclimation process with a dog that shows any signs. Your veterinarian may be able to prescribe a motion-sickness drug in bad cases.

Show puppies should become accustomed to traveling in the car in their crates, since this will be the likely method of travel to dog shows. Do not give the puppy water while in the crate. Remember to accustom the puppy to shorter trips before attempting a long ride. Happy trails.

The safest means of travel for dogs is in a crate. Show dogs especially need to become accustomed to traveling in this fashion.

WMK·732

GROOMING

Even if your puppy does not belong to a race of high-maintenance canines, you still need to accustom him to grooming. Grooming here means more than standing still while the professional groomer buzzes away at your Poodle's pompadour. Grooming involves clipping the nails, brushing and combing the coat, checking the ears, feet, teeth, and eyes, bathing on occasion, and a regular once-over for fleas and ticks.

Make grooming time quality time with your puppy. If he belongs to one of "those" breeds, you'll really need to work on expanding his concentration and patience for the process. Besides the ever-elaborate Poodle, many breeds, especially if you are considering showing the dog, will need considerable grooming time. In the waiting room of the beauty salon you'll find the Bichon

Frise, Lhasa Apso, Shih Tzu, Chow Chow, Maltese, Collie, Samoyed, most terrier breeds, and many others.

If you have a dog that is small enough to groom on a table, purchase a specially designed grooming table or use another similarly sized table. Be sure the top is nonskid so that the puppy feels secure and won't slide off. Accustom the puppy to laying on his side to be brushed. Fortunately most of the more dominant breeds don't have high-maintenance coats, and most of the high-maintenance breeds have a natural tolerance for all the fussing.

Get the dog used to having his feet touched. Check his ears for wax build-up. Go over his coat for parasites, burrs, and the like. Nail clipping is every dog's recurrent nightmare, next to bathing! Introduce the dog to his new friend, the nail clipper (the guillotine type is

recommended). If you've gotten the puppy used to having his feet touched beforehand, this will be an easier battle. Hold his feet and kiss his toes. Tell him he's good and

The Afghan Hound is a real handful to groom. Afghans possess nearly humanlike hair that requires regular attention. Accustom the high-maintenance puppy to grooming from an early age.

beautiful. Let him sniff the clipper. Take the point off one nail—just the point or else he will bleed. (Having a styptic handy is not a bad idea, but you should have no concern if you take off just the very tip of the nail.) Tell him he's wonderful after he's let you clip the nail. If he isn't going bananas, try the second nail. If you've gotten this far, call it a day. Continue on the next eight a couple days later. By the end of the week, he'll have his first fabulous manicure! Week two can be devoted to his pedicure.

Time to brush his teeth. Yes, these are modern times and we do brush our dogs' teeth. Get the puppy used to having his mouth touched. If you plan to show the dog, accustom him to having a judge look inside his mouth to check his bite—and maybe to count his teeth. Therefore, he needs all his teeth, so let's keep

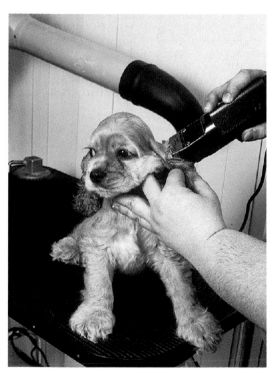

them clean and bright. Your veterinarian or pet shop can offer you a doggy toothbrush (arched and soft) and toothpaste for dogs (never human toothpaste).

Cocker Spaniels will visit the grooming salon as often as any other dog. Well-socialized puppies will enjoy the attention and look forward to grooming time.

Introduce the brush to the dog. Then put the toothpaste on. He'll think the toothpaste is food otherwise and attempt to lick it off the brush. Inevitably, dogs will help you along with their tongues as you attempt to brush their teeth. This is work, not fun. While it's okay for the dog to enjoy your time with him, he must also be serious about the work at hand. You don't want the dog chomping down on the brush, or your hand. Brush up and down, and don't

Brushing teeth is not optional, for you or your dog. A weekly brushing will help keep his smile pearly white.

Some sporting-breed puppies have more coat than you might think. This English Springer Spaniel pup is being groomed for a puppy match.

forget the back of the teeth. Praise him during the process and then give

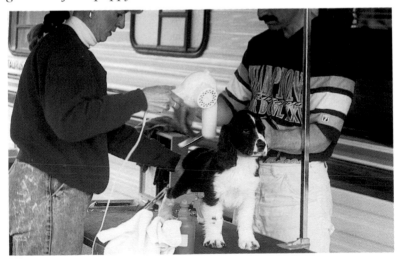

him a pat and a Nylabone® for his reward.

Approach bathing with caution as some dogs truly despise getting wet in a tub or basin. Of course these same dogs love to romp through mud puddles, necessitating the bath in the first place.

Unless you have a retriever or water dog, most dogs don't like being wet. Be efficient but thorough when bathing. A squeaky clean dog is a happy dog.

Introduce the puppy to the bathroom or whichever room you'll use. If it's a warm day, outside may be a good option. Unless you're reacting to a mud puddle, skunk, or some other mess, you may opt to not give the bath upon this first introduction to the room. Let the puppy sit in the basin. Make the experience fun. Take pictures. Sit and talk to him. When you're ready to take the plunge and actually give him a bath, use a hose to expedite the process. No sense making this the Ring Cycle of baths.

Don't be talked out of bathing your dog. Although a bath isn't needed daily, frequent baths really do not harm a dog's coat.

Have your shampoo ready. Wet him down, shampoo, and be sure to get the suds out, as soap in the coat will lead to irritation. Have towels ready. And one for you.

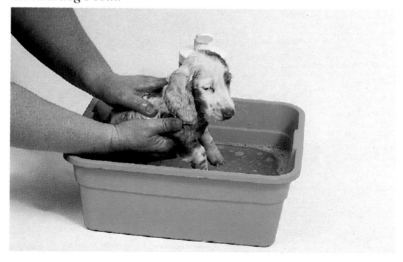

GLAMOROUS Life of Dogs

For a new puppy owner who is not a "dog person," the world of dogs may be a mystery. Dog people do not just own dogs. Their dogs are intrinsically attached to their ambitions, goals, and happiness. Breeding, training, and showing dogs comprise a whole world that invites you and your puppy to explore and experience. Many of the activities described here are designed to accommodate the purebred dog, though some activities can be enjoyed by mixed breed and purebred dogs alike.

The Super Bowl of dogs, the Westminster Kennel Club Dog Show takes place annually in New York City and has since 1877. This is the most prestigious American show and the second oldest sporting event in the U.S.

DOG SHOWS occur on practically every weekend of the year, depending on where you live. Dog people don't think much of driving eight hours to a dog show or flying a few hundred miles to an important show. Shows range from an all-breed show (up to 150 breeds) to a single-breed show, called a specialty. Specialties are geared to one breed, though sometimes a group of dogs is involved. Dog shows can have as many as 5000 dogs competing or as few as five. The largest dog show in the world is the Crufts dog show, held annually in Birmingham, England. Over four days, about 20,000 champion dogs are exhibited.

A family of Shih Tzu preparing for the day's competition: what price glamour? Braids, bows, and long hours of primping. "Primp, primp, primp...but we're naturally beautiful!"

At a dog show, each dog is judged against a standard of perfection, a written description of what the ideal specimen of his breed should look like. These standards are created by the parent club and adopted by the sponsoring kennel club. Although it looks like the dogs are being judged against one another, they are actually being judged against the standard. Dogs shows are sometimes called conformation shows, because each dog must "conform" to the standard. A dog must be chosen over a certain number of dogs of his breed at a certain number of dog shows in order to gain a championship. The qualifications for a championship vary from kennel club to kennel club, as well as from country to country.

To get your puppy used to the show ring, bring him to an outdoor show or match (practice show). This is great socialization and will give you a taste of the dog sport as well. Breeders and handlers there will readily take time to answer questions or to just talk "dogs" with you.

OBEDIENCE TRIALS have become increasingly popular and involve both purebred dogs and mixed breeds. Formal obedience classes can help prepare you and your puppy to participate in these competitions. The exercises range from the basic sit and down to more advanced scent discrimination work, a long jump, and retrieving a dumbbell. There is nothing more pleasurable than seeing your puppy grow up into an obedience contender, obeying your commands with precision and willingness. Obedience classes are offered in most areas of the country. These are a great place to start off to see how amenable and enthusiastic your puppy is to obedience.

An obedience trial is underway as these four competitors prepare to execute the long sit.

A multi-talented multi-titled Cocker Spaniel takes the broad jump: this is Ch. Sandor's Dutch Chocolate, UDTX, owned by Judy Iby.

The Papillon showing off its good nose and good sense....in scent discrimination this is Marsan Marshalik Am-Can. UD.

FIELD TRIALS are geared toward the hunting breeds like the Labrador and Golden Retrievers, Pointers, Beagles, Spaniels, and Coonhounds.

The most intense of field trials are those for retriever breeds. Field trials are an expensive and time-consuming activity. Relatively few field trial champions are awarded yearly.

These trials attempt to simulate a hunting environment. The most common trials are those in which retrievers compete. Field trials are not for the casual fancier as they are very competitive and costly. Training for field trials involves a daily commitment to working with the dog. While there are wonderful accounts of owners who have trained their dogs in a nearby mud puddle, owners ideally need a body of water and considerable land to train the dogs properly. While many non-retrievers have excelled in retrieving, your chances with a Labrador or Golden Retriever by far exceed the possibilities you'd have with a

Poodle or Rottweiler, no matter how talented the dog.

Consider a less intense avenue for your dashing retriever. At a fun trial, this Chesapeake Bay Retriever retrieves a pigeon.

TRACKING is a sport that tests a dog's ability to follow a scented trail. Many breeds compete in tracking, though the Bloodhound has no peer in the sport. From Rottweilers to Chihuahuas, the sport can be enjoyable for most any dog. The tests are fairly involved, covering various types of terrain and recreating specific situations. To reach the highest level, a dog must be a specialist in scent discrimination and following a trail.

A similar but non-competitive activity for a tracking dog is known as search and rescue. SAR dogs assist in searches for persons lost after an avalanche, flood, or other natural catastrophe. Newfoundlands and St. Bernards, as well as Golden and Labrador Retrievers and German Shepherds, are the more popular breeds trained for work in this field.

Dogs are also employed in narcotics, arson, and weapon searches. Bloodhounds, Beagles, and retrievers are used in these pursuits. While these are not activities or sports as such, they do represent the abilities and natural talents that dogs have

Kiwi is an avalanche rescue worker....this is putting tracking to the test and maybe saving a person's life. The handler is Fay Johnson.

Who tossed the mop over the bar jump? This talented agility dog is a Puli, one of the brightest little canines in the world.

and demonstrate how they use them.

AGILITY TRIALS are the hottest new event in the dog world. These trials look like obstacle courses and require a dog and his handler to work closely while maneuvering their way through. While the sport is still being standardized, the most commonly seen obstacles are the A-frame, dog walk, tunnel, weave poles, and seesaw. These are exciting trials for man and dog, and spectator too. Training for these competitions requires a great commitment, not to mention the right equipment. Many different breeds participate in these trials,

The Dalmatian is tireless...and through the tire jump he goes!

which started in Great Britain and have swept the United States and Canada with great enthusiasm. The presence of the Border Collie cannot be missed in these events, although most every breed has been represented, from the tall, elegant Saluki to the tiny Yorkshire Terrier. Of course the obstacles are

Over the wall goes a yellow Labrador Retriever at an agility trial. Labradors excel in agility just as they do in obedience and field trials.

appropriately adjusted for the height of the dogs competing.

SHEEPDOG TRIALS today keep many of our working sheepdogs in shape. Ironically, the trials were designed to improve a sheepdog's ability. Now the trials help keep the dogs in shape and their instincts sharp. In England, where these trials are very popular, they are televised and boast large audiences. The most common contenders at sheepdog trials are Border Collies, Australian Shepherds, and Australian Cattle Dogs, though any number of herding dogs participate. Like agility and obedience trials, these trials involve the handler as well as the dog. The handler moves the dog with hand signals and whistles. In America these are called Herding Tests and are not nearly as exciting as the British equivalent sheepdog trials.

Schutzhund has more to offer than a ripped sleeve. This German Shepherd is participating in the traffic section of a Schutzhund test.

SCHUTZHUND is a German sport that gained acceptance in the United States for a time. It involves teaching protection dogs how to move among a restless crowd, search for felons, stop an intruder, voice a warning—and more. Obviously this sport is meant for certain breeds. Many trainers don't recommend intensifying the natural instincts of already aggressive dogs, such as Rottweilers or Doberman Pinschers. These breeds are naturally capable of guard work without specialized sleeve work and the like. Dogs with a Schutzhund degree are able track, protect, and perform obedience under stressful situations.

This Golden Retriever undergoes the Canine Good Citizen test. One requirement of the test is that the dog must react calmly to various distractions in its environment.

CANINE GOOD CITIZEN is an American certification program for dogs who demonstrate that they are well-behaved members of the community as well as good, trustworthy companions. A dog must pass a series of ten tests involving everyday, non-competitive situations. This program, sponsored by the American Kennel Club, is most welcome in the United States, a country which by and large is not dog-friendly. If every pet dog in the country gained its C.G.C. title, mutts, mongrels, and curs included, owners would become more conscientious dog people—and legislators would notice! Happily there would be less anti-dog legislation, and well-behaved dogs with their well-behaved owners would be allowed in more public places. It is surely an injustice to prohibit well-trained dogs from romping on the beach or strolling through a park or on a boardwalk. In a more perfect world, all of our "canine good citizens" would be welcome in public places, including restaurants, trains, and even churches. Americans should look to the Continent for examples in this regard. In Europe, dogs are far more accepted as members of society and the family, though this can become fanatical too; when dogs become more important than children, we know we have some reevaluating to do.

THERAPY DOGS are dogs who spend time in nursing home facilities, hospitals, prisons, etc., visiting with patients or inmates. It requires little more than a friendly dog and an owner's commitment to be certified to make the visits. Participants in these programs have so many wonderful stories to tell about their dogs and the good cheer and hope they bring to the patients. Pet therapy promises to be rewarding for everyone involved. More and more institutions have introduced these programs to their communities.

INSTINCT TESTS have been designed to test a dog's natural instincts, or in some cases to awaken a dog's dormant ones. There are hunting tests to engage sporting breeds that aren't actively involved in field trials;

Getting your dog involved with a therapy program is excellent socialization for your dog and a great way to contribute to the community. This Golden Retriever visits nursing homes all year long.

earthdog trials to entice the small terriers and Dachshund; lure coursing events to challenge the housebound Whippet and Saluki; sled pulling to harness the Huskies and Malamutes; coaching trials to step up Dalmatians; water tests to test water dogs, such as the Newfoundland and Portuguese Water Dog;

Getting back to nature, present-day owners are looking for ways to rediscover their dogs' lost pasts. This Australian Shepherd is herding ducks at an instinct test.

and herding tests to waken sleepy sheepdogs, who meet sheep, goats, and geese for the first time in the training sessions for these tests. These events are less intense than field trials and sheepdog trials and do not require as much training. In line with the current trends to return to Nature, with homeopathic medicine, miracles and mysticism, instinct tests for our dogs bring them into our New Age thinking.

"We're hunting wabbit!!" Two Beagles in hot pursuit at a field trial. Originally bred for rabbit and other small game, today's Beagle barely gets his nose wet when it comes to hunting.

VERSATILITY PROGRAMS

Each recognized breed in a kennel club has a parent club

organization that is dedicated to the protection and betterment of that breed. In recent years, parent clubs have issued new awards to promote versatility within the breed. Many breeders tend to concentrate on only one area of the dog sport, such as conformation shows, and not attempt to title the dog in obedience or another field. Dual championships,

Versatility aptly describes the Golden Retriever. This young pup acquaints himself with a training decoy. Breeder, Dr. Kaye Fuller. Photograph courtesy of Nona Kilgore Bauer.

which combine conformation and field trial championships, have become increasingly scarce in recent years, and few triple championships (conformation, field, and obedience trial championships) have ever been won.

Of course certain breeds are more naturally versatile than others. The sporting dogs have won more dual championships than all other breeds combined. Other breeds, such as the German Shepherd Dog, Border Collie, and Poodle, have won more than one championship title.

As has been seen in breeds like the Labrador and Golden Retriever, breed type tends to vary when

The German Shepherd's talents have been redirected toward new tasks. While moving sheep is no longer one of his daily chores, he does protect, detect, lead, deliver and rescue.

breeders concentrate on only one area of competition. Dogs bred solely for the show ring tend to become exaggerated in bone or coat; dogs bred solely for field have become racy and whippety. The versatility awards are an attempt to reglue the bridge between the two types. The extreme examples seen in the two popular retrievers have made breeders and judges aware of how important versatility in a breed truly is. Among the breeds that can celebrate their original bred-for capacities are the Border Collie, Australian Kelpie and Cattle Dog, Pointer, Flat-Coated Retriever, Chesapeake Bay Retriever, Curly-Coated Retriever, Brittany, and certainly many others.

Still an instinctual herder, the Australian Shepherd has become a top choice for a family dog and show dog, especially if acquired from an up and coming breeder like Caterina O'Sullivan.

Unfortunately a good number of the breeds that were once class working dogs have become one-dimensional show dogs. The Collie, Shetland Sheepdog, Beagle, and most terrier breeds no longer function in their born-for capacities. Of course, technology has put dogs out of work for centuries—inventions like the wheel, firearms, snowmobiles, fire trucks, electric alarm systems, etc.—and, when these dogs' talents were no longer needed, they either became extinct or were embraced as pets. Fortunately the new trend of instinct tests has renewed interest in seeing many of these talented specialists back at work doing their "thing."

SUGGESTED READING

BY THE AUTHOR

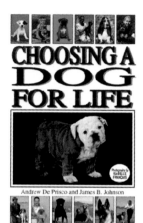

Andrew De Prisco and James B. Johnson

TS-257
Choosing A Dog For Life

Every owner's first choice for a selection handbook, illustrated with over 700 full-color photographs, this authoritative volume discusses the standards, health, growth, special needs, temperament and training of the most popular 166 dog breeds. Representing the first-hand experience and advice of hundreds of dedicated breeders and owners, this definitive and beautiful book is absolutely essential for anyone looking for a purebred dog.

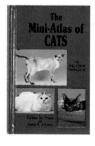

H-1106
The Mini-Atlas of Dog Breeds

Over 400 breeds presented in color with descriptions of each breed's history, portrait, and temperament. A handy sized field guide to the international world of dogs and the most accurate and entertaining source of its kind. Over 500 color photographs on 544 pages.

TS-152
The Mini-Atlas of Cats

Cat breeds presented in full color with descriptions of each cat's temperament, needs, physical appearance, as well as likes and dislikes. A thoroughly amusing browse through the cat world illustrated with nearly 500 fabulous photographs.

TS-175
The Most Complete Dog Book Ever Published: A Canine Lexicon

Over 3500 alphabetically arranged entries present over 500 breeds of dog and related topics of breeding, showing, anatomy, health care... includes over 1300 color photographs on 896 pages. Guaranteed to live up to its not so modest title!

INDEX

Accommodations, 30, 54–55
Aggression, 110
Aggressive puppy, 20
Agility trials, 150
Airedale Terrier, 36, 128
Alaskan Malamute, 130
Akita, 15,36,112
American Pit Bull Terrier, 112, 121
Anti-freeze, 32
Argentine Dogo, 112
Astrology, 68
Attention span, 71
Australian Cattle Dog, 124
Automobiles, 134
Barking, 98
Basenji, 101
Basic commands, 79-87
Basset Hound, 101
Bathing, 142
Beagle, 101, 128
Begging, 105
Behavior modification, 88
Bernese Mountain Dog, 128
Biting, 94
Body language, 75, 122
Bonding, 29
Border Collie, 124
Bowl stand, 55
Bowls, 54
Boxer, 55

Breeders, 26, 28
Breeds, 59
Brittany, 128
Brushes, 56
Bull and terrier breeds, 112
Bulldog, 15, 124
Bullmastiff, 112,124
Canine Good Citizen, 153
Cars, 134
Carsickness, 137
Cesarean section, 15
Chase, 43
Chewing, 96
Chihuahua, 15
Chow Chow, 101
Christmas, 31
Collar, 56
Combs, 56
Come, 40, 81
Commands, 79-87
Conformation shows, 144
Coonhound, 101
Correction, 20–21, 72, 74, 110
Crate, 46, 54
Crate training, 46–47
—mistakes, 53
—schedule, 51–52
Crazies, 109
Crossbreeds, 68
Crufts Dog Show, 25, 144
Crying, 91
Dalmatian, 49
Dam, 14, 15, 26
Digging, 116

Discipline, 21, 70
Doberman Pinscher, 112, 126
Dog shows, 144
Dogue de Bordeaux, 124
Dominance, 20, 110
Dominant down, 21
Down, 84
Drop it, 87
English Mastiff, 30
Enough, 86
Expectations, 22
Father, 14, 26
Fear period, 90
Fetch, 42
Field trials, 126, 148
Finnish Spitz, 101
Flyball, 132
Food, 56
Food rewards, 77
Frisbee®, 42
Furniture, 106
German Shepherd, 15, 124
Giant Schnauzer, 128
Golden Retriever, 126
Great Dane, 55
Greyhounds, 66
Grooming, 138
Growling, 21
Gundogs, 64
Heel, 81
Here, 87
Home safety, 31
Hounds, 65
Housebreaking, 16, 46–53, 128

Huskies, 63, 130
Identification, 57
Instinct tests, 154
Instincts, 124
Intelligence, 118
Jumping on
    furniture, 106
Jumping up, 103
Keeshond, 15
Komondor, 112
Labrador Retrievers,
    126
Language, 120, 122
Lassie, 25, 26
Leadership, 17
Leash, 56
Leash training, 37
Lifting leg, 38
Mastiffs, 62, 126
Microchip, 57
Miniature Schnauzer,
    127
Misbehavior, 19
Mother, 14, 15, 26
Multiple-dog
    household, 36
Mutts, 68
Nails, 139
Name, 75
Natural breeds, 15
New Guinea Singing
    Dog, 98
Night, 87
Nipping, 94
No, 33
Nylabone®, 56, 95,
Obedience trials, 146
Off, 85
OK, 85

Out, 87
Pack instinct, 17
Paper training, 48–
    50
Papillon, 126, 127
Parenthood, 22
Pit Bull Terrier, 36
Play, 40
Poodle, 124
Punishment, 72
Puppy gate, 55
Puppy-proofing, 31
Responsibility, 10
Retrievers, 64
Rewards, 77
Rottweiler, 112,126
Running wild, 108
Saint Bernard, 55
Scenthounds, 65,
    101
Schutzhund, 152
Schwartz, Charlotte,
    132
Scruff shake, 21
Selection, 68
Selective hearing,
    121
Sexual maturity, 90
Shaker-can, 74
Shampoo, 56
Sheepdog trials, 152
Sheepdogs, 61, 124
Shetland, 15, 101
Sheepdog, 124
Shiba Inu, 121, 131
Show puppy, 23
Siberian Husky, 130
Sighthounds, 66, 128
Sire, 14, 26

Sit, 79
Sit-stay, 80
Sleep, 87
Socialization, 18, 27
Spitz, 63
Sporting dogs, 64
Stand, 83
Standard, 145
Structured time, 36
Submission, 22
Submissive urination,
    117
Supplements, 56
Tattoo, 57
Teeth, 90, 140
Terriers, 60, 127
Therapy dogs, 154
Thinking, 118
Tone of voice, 76,
    123
Toy dogs, 67
Tracking, 149
–initial, 33
–leash, 37
Traveling, 134
Tug of war, 42
Versatility programs,
    156
Veterinarian, 57
Vizsla, 128
Wait, 86
Walk, 87
Weimaraner, 55
Westminster Kennel
    Club, 14, 25
Wetting, 117
Whippet, 15
Wolf, 15